Charles —

As an Effective leader
you will enjoy
Reading This Book —

Jerry

Praise for
SIDE B

"Motivational and memorable; focusing and energizing—these are the characteristics of great music *and* great leaders. In *Side B,* Paula White creates a clever and apt framework that blends both and informs it with stories, examples, and interviews with sales professionals, musicians, and other experts. It's time to rehumanize business by blending in our B-sides."

—**Ethan Beute**, Chief Evangelist at BombBomb and Host of "The Customer Experience Podcast"

"Paula White has the heart of a writer, the brain of a leader, and the instinct of a teacher. This book has the potential to create success on so many levels. Crack it open and prove me right."

—**Bonnie J. Baker**, Songwriter; Producer and Owner, bker MGMT

"*Side B* provides a great reminder for all readers: organizational charts are filled with humans, and engaging our humanity is a strength, not a weakness, in developing as a leader."

—**David Scheaf**, Assistant Professor of Entrepreneurship, Baylor University

"*Side B* is a must-read for anyone seeking to return to their authentic self and break free of the 'echo chamber.' Read this book to learn how to reconnect with your authenticity through music."

—**David Stine**, Northeast Region Sales Director; U.S. Air Force Major (Retired)

"Tapping into music as your leadership muse is such an inspired and clever concept! *Side B* challenges us to tie the passions we have for music into how we lead and guides us on how to do it. WARNING: you might not be able to get certain songs out of your head after reading!"

—**Jennifer J Fondrevay**, M&A Thought Leader;
Founder of Day1 Ready; Bestselling
Author of *Now What?*

"Paula has explored the concepts of authentic leadership, emotional intelligence, vulnerability and music in this book. Side B will no doubt provide readers an opportunity to stop, breathe and reflect on their own Side B of untapped brilliance!"

—**Michelle Redfern**, Advancing Women
in Business and Sport

"I would have read this book early in my leadership career and paid much more attention to Side B...of those I was leading and my own."

—**Karen Moriarty**, Principal Consultant

"*Side B* helped me unearth a little part of me I'd forgotten about. Paula's writing teaches you how to bring your best self–your WHOLE self–to the people you lead and the people you love. I'm ten songs into my 'Power Up' playlist, and it WORKS. When I hit play, I'm ready to bravely take on whatever is in front of me."

—**Michele Kelly**, Co-founder of K+L Storytellers,
contributing author to *GoldenHeart II:
We Are Your Family, Today's Inspired Leader*
and *81 Words Anthology*

"A book that transcends across many professions in business, education, the arts, and life experiences. In *Side B: Remix Your Leadership Style*, Paula White invites us to open ourselves up to being human—the best part of who we truly are. Music becomes more than a metaphor; it transforms us into our 'authentic self' and gives us an opportunity to explore our emotions."

—Deborah Morbitt Ph.D., Educator

"Before reading *Side B*, I had never thought of the messages in my head as a powerful soundtrack influencing every aspect of my life—including my effectiveness as a leader. Paula White shares how to change that soundtrack to work for you, not against you, and how to uncover and develop your 'Side B tracks' to reach your full potential as a leader."

—Julie Hansen, Author, *Look Me In the Eye*

"*Side B* is the type of book that appeals to new and experienced leaders alike. Paula has a unique perspective on leadership and bringing your full self to work that is both easy to follow and thought-provoking. As a seasoned (see old) leader, I was particularly drawn to Paula's commentary on legacy (with each person you interact with, you leave your legacy) and the disconnection so many of us feel in "a world hungry to be heard." Leaders carry a responsibility to bring their full self to each interaction, and *Side B* provides practical advice to do just that."

—John Healy, Vice President, Sales & Marketing at DDI

"*Side B* challenges the 'norm' when it comes to the leadership behaviors needed to thrive and develop phenomenal, high-performing teams in today's corporate space. Challenge yourself to 'make the flip' and check out Paula's refreshing take on making the most of your abilities."

—Juli Lassow, Owner & Principal, JHL Solutions

Side B

Remix Your Leadership Style

Paula S. White

MADE FOR
SUCCESS

Made for Success Publishing
P.O. Box 1775 Issaquah, WA 98027
www.MadeForSuccessPublishing.com

Distributed by Made for Success Publishing

First Printing

Library of Congress Cataloging-in-Publication data
White, Paula S.
        SIDE B: Remix Your Leadership Style
            p. cm.

LCCN: 2021942397
ISBN: 978-1-64146-674-5 (*Hardback*)
ISBN: 978-1-64146-675-2 (*eBook*)
ISBN: 978-1-64146-676-9 (*Audiobook*)

Printed in the United States of America

For further information contact Made for Success Publishing
+14255266480 or email service@madeforsuccess.net

CONTENTS

FOREWORD

Paula and I met several years ago at a leadership conference, and I was immediately impressed with her
résumé, boasting a successful career as a business developer
and upcoming leader. However, it wasn't just her accolades that drew me to her; it was her character and heart.
Fortunately, our paths crossed again a few ago as Paula
was on her self-awareness journey, pivoting to focus on her
Authentic Leadership Legacy: combining her résumé skills
with her people skills. As we spent hours talking on Zoom
calls, Paula thoughtfully explained her unique approach to
enabling emerging and senior leaders through this same
pivot she had just made.

We agreed on many thought-provoking themes around
leadership development, but most specifically on developing
paradoxical balances between action-oriented and supportive
behaviors. At one point, Paula announced to me that she was

working on an upcoming book, and I was intrigued with and invested in her unique approach.

As I thought about her passion and how she described the relationship between music, Side B behaviors, and her leadership development approach, Paula inspired me to engage others to talk about their experiences with music at different times of their lives and how it touched them emotionally.

As I became more enthusiastic about how to coach/mentor a multi-generational workforce, and as we focused on senior *and* emerging leaders, I was provided an opportunity to read Paula's finished book.

With extensive experience in multiple careers and industries, I reached executive roles as a manager and leader. I have spent many years coaching and mentoring others as they transition into leadership roles. However, it wasn't until reading *Side B* that what I had felt all along became clear. I realized that both Side A and Side B behaviors are imperative to success. It also became apparent that developing a high level of balanced versatility between these behaviors is what enables us to build healthier relationships. Paula has, without a doubt, inspired and motivated me as I "turned my music back on."

Paula has developed an innovative approach that applies music to business success and humanity to encourage engagement, courage, and authenticity by developing our Side B. She envisions an environment where everyone is seen and heard while still achieving extraordinary results. By using music as a foundation, a universal language, leaders tap into their authentic leadership language and positive behavior traits to serve the people they lead.

Paula's approach with musical instruments as a way to uncover unique leadership styles is incredibly creative and insightful and empowers us to take a deep dive as we continue becoming the leader we want to be. If you will take the opportunity to absorb and implement Paula's creative methodology, you will see massive results in both the people you lead and the person looking back at you in the mirror.

—*Jerry Scher*, Managing Partner for Peak Focus, LLC, and Harrison™ Assessments

PREFACE

Sometimes, you must travel down the wrong road to find the right one. Metaphorically speaking, my "wrong road" zig-zagged me around the world twice to finally write the book you now hold in your hands.

Three years ago, I started writing my manuscript. I thought that if I shared my story and explained my mistakes, both in business and in my personal life, then you would have a clearer path to self-awareness as a leader. The problem seemed straightforward, or so I thought. As leaders, we try to emulate someone else or what we believe is the "right" way to lead. I did this for an exceptionally long time; three decades invested in the myth that to be a great leader, you have to work nonstop, keep your emotions in check, stay focused on the prize, and lead from your head rather than your heart.

My career did not lack this approach.

I became good at transforming inside sales teams into multi-million-dollar stand-alone sales channels while achieving 8 to 10% compounded yearly growth within veterinary and healthcare distribution. I was honored with the Regional Manager of the Year and Top Team Outstanding Achievements awards. I became a member of the AA-ISP Advisory Board and was named a "Top 25 Most Influential Sales Leader" for three consecutive years by AA-ISP. In 2017, I was awarded the Excellence in Execution award by AA-ISP, ranked in the "Top 100 Coaches to Watch" for two consecutive years by Ambition.

But all of these accomplishments came with a price. Being a textbook workaholic for years led to the confusion of my priorities, inconsistency in my attitude, uncertainty of my feelings, and burnout—all at great personal cost to my health, sleep, and family.

I knew that I could not go on without making significant changes. My starting point? To understand the path that landed me there, where I went wrong, and the boxes I checked (and the boxes I put myself in) to earn the titles I thought I needed in order to be a great leader.

Here, at a very low point in my life, knowing this was a path I could no longer stay on, I decided to begin my "research." How could I be the extraordinary leader I was meant to be AND have balance in my life, feel energized and whole, and leave a legacy for decades to come? So, I went out on a journey to speak with 19 CEOs, executive coaches, mentors, and experts in business. I either flew to meet them in person for an interview or, with COVID-19, held Zoom meetings to get their professional viewpoints for the book. I planned to highlight each professional to help you, wise reader, become a little wiser. I wanted to share my story and help you build skills around topics like mentoring, entrepreneurship, leadership, failure, and listening. I was even able to get perspectives on the differences between women and men in leadership roles—something that has always fascinated me. Through this adventure, I came back with a fuller grasp of what makes a great leader.

I quickly wrote the first four chapters, and they were solid. However, I found myself stuck trying to complete the remaining four chapters. I kept reading what I had written over and over again. (Amazingly, I still thought they sounded surprisingly good!) Then the lightbulb moment came. I was using *their* words to *write* my book because I couldn't share my own. I wasn't ready to be vulnerable.

Trust me on this: that was not the book I wanted to write, nor the one you needed to read. The truth was that my words were not powerful enough. A song I created called "Who Wants to Hear Me?" played in an endless loop in my head. Here I was, writing a book about authentic leadership, and I was borrowing the words and ideas of others. Through every conversation I had, I started to realize that the part of me that needed to show up was being asked to sit quietly on the sidelines. I didn't trust her voice, her thoughts, or her as "chief muse" in my approach.

That part of me was what you'll learn later as Side B, that second-best song no one ever expected to be a hit on the back of 45 rpm records. She was always buried inside me.

WOW. Take that in for a moment.

I was trying too hard to be something I am not, and, in that moment, I realized my song was not finished.

So, I trashed the entire book. All 50,000 words of it.

The writing was cathartic and opened my creative mind to what I truly wanted to say—what had been there this whole time. In this book, the one you are holding and the one I knew was right, we will go on a journey together. We will look at the power of music to reframe your leadership style and, ultimately, the leadership legacy you are remembered by. We will learn about balanced behaviors and how they can enhance your God-given competencies and traits. We will journey through lessons that will teach you how to create a corporate environment of accountability, encouragement, and kindness.

Music is not only a metaphor but also a tool to understand your Side B behaviors—those lesser-known but no less important attributes you possess as a leader. I will show you how creating a playlist with your own musical tastes can bring out your unique style of leadership and legacy that will not only be impactful to yourself and your teams but drive results and company growth.

So, how the heck do we do this? Well, first, we must aim for a balance defined by our résumé-based skills and competencies and what we will call our Side B behaviors and traits, which are emotion-based. These emotion-based traits are rarely represented but leave a lasting impression on the people you serve. It is within those balanced skills, competencies, traits, and behaviors that we are able to bring our **ALL** (*Authentic Leadership Legacy*) to create a team culture where people are excited to work together and support one another, the organization (especially in terms of healthier topline and bottom-line growth), and provide an amazing customer experience. Finally, it is critical to your own sense of life fulfillment because giving the best of you to the people you lead is one of the most satisfying feelings of all.

Here's the thing: This is doable. Exploring your Side B doesn't take a considerable time commitment. Most leaders are time-starved and travel-weary, and that's *before* unexpected events pop up. (Thankfully, tapping into your Side B leadership traits will help you utilize the resources you already have.) Yet, it is one of the most profound transformations you can make for an authentic leadership legacy.

So, what are you waiting for? No regrets. No time to spare. Let's get to it.

CHAPTER 1

MUSIC IS EVERYWHERE,
SO WHY NOT IN LEADERSHIP?

"Music is not in the notes,
but in the silence between."
—*Wolfgang Amadeus Mozart*

Meet Henry.[1] You might recognize him. He is sitting in his office well after 8 p.m., and he probably went home for dinner, then returned to the office to catch up on his work. It's dark out, and you can see the glow of his desk lamp and the dim reflection of his computer screen from the street.

Henry is the leader and CEO of a mid-sized privately held organization; however, he also represents the CEOs of many growing organizations. He is strong in his business acumen and can dissect a P&L with as much ease as scientists who

---

[1] Fictional name.

can recognize and name each element on the periodic table without fail. He is faced with daily tasks, appointments, and decisions, but most often, he sits alone in his office. His time is like a chessboard—each move must be calculated, and pawns may need to be sacrificed to reach the end goal. He is fully aware that people are counting on him to grow the company x times market, to achieve results while minimizing costs, mistakes, and crises. He feels like an octopus being stretched in eight different directions. And tomorrow, the game starts all over.

♪♪♪

I believe some leaders tend to forget what it is like to be themselves. They lose sight of their own uniqueness and what earned them that title, role, leadership position, seat at the table, or that big, bright corner office. I wonder if Henry is aware of the legacy he is leaving with the people in his organization. I knew him at a time in our lives when having a conversation with him was delightful and impactful. We would strategize on the next sales incentive, review results, and plan our next growth opportunity. Henry and I knew how to hold a conversation; it was fun when he would dress in the spirit of holidays like a fun rock 'n' roll character for Halloween, Santa in December, and in his favorite team colors during March

Madness with a mischievous grin on his face. I want to walk up to his office this minute and tell him to be himself again, but I am afraid that I will disrupt an important meeting, or even worse, get that look telling me, "We have better things to do in the workplace, get at it."

I have had my fair share of experiences with extraordinary, great, good, and not-so-good leaders over the past 30 years. Here's what I've learned: Success truly comes down to who you are as an *authentic* leader when you are in those precious and coveted seats within the organization. Yet, when we reach the top of the corporate ladder, that is precisely when we often stop looking inward and forget about the importance of self-awareness and individuality.

Henry could be an extraordinary leader. Extraordinary leaders continuously study their craft, understand where they can get better, and also acknowledge who they really are as a leader (and who they are not). Leadership becomes a practice, no different than practicing scales on a piano. You must understand that a leader's starring role, then, is not about the job or title but rather about the work they do for the people they *serve.* It is about their authentic behavior at every step in their career, understanding that their unique gifts can motivate and inspire others, leaving a legacy that goes far beyond their business accolades.

If your heart shifted reading those words, here's the question I pose to you: If being an extraordinary leader depends on your self-awareness journey, then what type of behavior are you leading with? It's OK if you don't know. Most people don't. Let's take a couple steps back and look at what brought you to this moment.

WHO TURNED OFF THE MUSIC?

Music defines the timeline and memories of our lives. The songs our mother sang to us at night, the music we did homework to in grade school, the song we danced to at our high school prom, the music we blasted on the radio in the first car we ever bought (mine was a red Maverick!), the first dance at our wedding. And then? Using music as a milestone marker trails off. We get busy. We rise up the ranks, and our focused time takes over. Creativity gives way to problem-solving. We live a life of triage, but we get the promotions and the salary hikes and the recognition. Unfocused dreaming becomes a luxury, or relegated to a long weekend here or there at the lake. In other words, leading means doing, accomplishing, and making things happen.

Today, there's no time for you to take off your leadership hat and let people get to know you—who you truly are and what makes you human. While we are working our way up the corporate ladder, we have turned off the music and begun listening to talk radio, sports on the radio, or podcasts to and from work. While all those tap into our interests, they don't allow for full expression of ourselves and the freedom music can bring, especially when it comes to our emotions.

Spending eight to ten hours a day at work with no outlet for creativity has led to attrition, but more importantly, to silence. Yes, technology has given rise to more efficiency and a do-it quicker attitude; however, there is more pressure, and we are losing the art of communication and caring. When my grandmother would go to work and sit at a sewing machine every day, at least she still had the opportunity to talk and laugh with her co-workers during the shift (and take an actual lunch break to sit down and catch up with them!).

The balance between focusing on mental health and the corporate world being so hierarchical is challenging. Since the fast-paced era of technology has increased corporate efficiency, many people have become like machines at work. More is expected of both leaders and employees. However, in recent years, I've noticed that those entering the workforce now seem to be leading a revolution to re-humanize the mindset and be open to emotions. Why wouldn't we expect this? They were brought up with movies like the *Harry Potter* series or *The Hunger Games*, both portraying the gift of fighting for the good of the people.

As leaders, you must be aware of this shift. Take notice when someone is walking by your desk over and over again. This is where you need to step into your whole self and take the time to acknowledge their humanness and ask how they're doing. As a whole, people in the workplace feel overwhelmed, underappreciated, and that they no longer matter. It's time to change this perspective, and, in turn, your teams will be more productive, and people will be more engaged, work harder, and support the organization because their leaders were gracious enough to just *listen* and show that they care.

As CEOs/leaders, we generally only focus on the bottom line and getting the most from our teams—that is just the name of the game. However, to truly achieve the results we long to see, we need to exhibit behaviors like trustworthiness, curiosity, kindness, and optimism—not just the practical leadership skills.

It is important to start *now.* Meaning today.

So, what does this have to do with music, exactly?

Well, in this case, music first helps us recognize those spaces in our minds that are jumbled with self-talk and reintroduces us to emotions that have likely been turned off on our climb up the corporate ladder. As we tune into our emotions and begin to see the people around us on an emotional level as well, music takes us from saying "I gotta do _____" to "I'm here as my whole self to be the best leader possible." It can also be as simple as the tempo, a lyric, or a powerful electric riff in a song that provides a dopamine hit and fuels the leader to be and do their best.

So, it's time to turn the music back on. We'll start by looking in the mirror and listening to the rhythm of… your heart.

SOLVING FOR THE SELF-AWARENESS GAP

Jack Welch, former CEO of General Electric, said, "Before you are a leader, success is all about growing yourself."

Growth starts within. To gain a clearer understanding of yourself, stop for a moment of silence and listen for your inner melody. In music, the symbol in a musical score prompting a pause or stop is called a fermata. In our everyday life, such an act often involves getting real and taking stock.

Everyone is unique, and until you are clear about your gifts, understand your potential pitfalls, and connect with who you are as a leader, you cannot fully serve others.

If you are shaking your head, saying, "Oh Paula. I know ALL about me. I'm a high C to a T!"[2] (Translation: highly analytical, as in, I will probably pick you to help me with my computer problem.) OK, so you might not be a closet personality "work-related" assessment-taker… or maybe you take every assessment you can in the hopes it will tell you something new. For me, it was the latter. I used to take every assessment possible, whether I was paying for it or searching for what was free on the web. I was looking for what boxes I checked and if the results laid out a plan for me to be a better leader.

Unfortunately, the answers only added to my confusion.

Assessments can be nerve-racking or freeing; it all depends on what it says or how the company interprets it on your behalf. The best thing I ever did was invest in an executive coach named Amy to help uncover who I am as a leader. Amy believes that assessments give you language to *support* your leadership skills rather than simply giving you a label in the form of a combination of numbers and letters or strengths.

[2] Disc Personality Test, https://www.test-guide.com/disc-personality -test.html

Nobody wants to be labeled; labels are limiting and can actually be incredibly deceiving.

Yes, I was the closet assessment taker looking for "The Answer" for what it took to be an extraordinary leader. Although, it wasn't until I hired Amy that I was truly open to reflection and beginning the journey to explore my own unique style of leadership—with the goal and intention to use it to serve people. Then, my goal became to learn how to apply the knowledge, as it is unique for every assessment instrument.

Hiring Amy, a professional coach *outside* my organization, allowed me to look in the mirror and face myself without fear or judgment. Taking assessments under the guidance of a professional helped me understand my gifts and where there was an opportunity for growth, and I gained so many valuable insights.

I learned (which allowed me to accept) that I rather enjoy analytics, processes, relationships, and innovation. I don't play in just one sandbox, or as I would say, I play more than one business instrument. I like to get my hands on all aspects of business and make them fit together to achieve the best results possible. The problem is, many see me as a scatterbrain who doesn't have a clear direction, which is the opposite of what is playing out in my head!

Amy and I took the time to organize my strengths and weaknesses so I was positioned to reach my full potential. This took nine months of intense reflection, and at first, I was unclear and resistant. Listen, I'm telling you it was tremendously difficult to truly focus on myself from the inside out, and there were wounds I needed to understand and heal, as my song did not start at the beginning of my career. However, it finally all came together when she outlined my uniqueness in a chart that explained my thinking style, my potential pitfalls, and my strengths. The more clarity and self-awareness I gained, the better I could serve those around me.

Of course, Amy was not my first mentor/coach. I can go back as far as my swim coach, Scott, who coached me from 5 to 12 years of age. Swimming competitively is a physical and mental grind. Not only are you up before dawn, hitting the pool, but you go back after school for more training. I was exercising every single muscle, including my brain!

There is something to be said about repetition in a swim lane, talking only to yourself and watching the black line pass with each stroke. I could feel the water breaking over my head as my arm strokes kept beat with my kicks, and I had to stay in tune with the rhythm of my heart beating so I could take a breath at just the right time to not lose momentum.

This was when the soundtrack of my life started to play in my head.

I heard tracks like "Keep Pushing Paula", "Am I Good Enough?", "Here They Come, Don't Let Them Pass" and the never-ending pulsating beat "Go, Go, I Am Almost There" only to immediately look up to see my results and time. Then that race was over, so it was on to the next.

What I didn't realize at the time was how those made-up songs would keep playing years later. Yet, I wasn't in the pool anymore; I was leading a team. What did that mean? I was still singing in my head, "Go, Go, We Are Almost There" and, before I knew it, each month became a race. All the while, I was searching for someone to help me uncover the "secret leadership language" I thought I needed to be the leader I was born to be.

But back to my coaching with Amy. Each assessment alone did not resonate with me; it wasn't until we put them all together that my eyes were opened to the power of music again. I began hearing my voice telling me, "It's time to grasp who you are as a leader." Yes, those assessments helped me to use specific attributes as an asset for everyday life and leadership. They can help you, too. However, they don't show us the whole picture. Remember, this is a journey to understanding your potential, and only you have the key to unlock the barriers to seeing it in its entirety. Learning how to unlock and utilize your Authentic Leadership Legacy is rewarding, freeing, *and* a lot of work. But it's worth it.

I found my inspiration again after realizing I had lost the sound and peace of music while working on my career. I remembered that I used to make mixtapes for different moods, playing songs in my head to recall information. With my dyslexia (a learning disorder and reading disability that affects the area of the brain that processes language; although today, after a lot of research and acceptance, it is simply known as neurodiversity), music helped me expand my vocabulary and articulate my thoughts. As my brain was processing language differently, music empowered, motivated, and inspired my self-confidence. Music allowed me to become creative and feel something in the moment.

Now, when I'm unclear in my direction, I turn on some music to help provide the insight I'm missing. Because there is no judgment in music, I am able to gain a lot of clarity on my leadership style through it. We don't have to answer to music. It is personal and allows us to hear and see what we need to gain clarity for ourselves. Think about it: When you're listening to the radio in the shower, on a walk, or in your car, your mind is free to explore your own thoughts because no one is judging them.

So, there we have it: the beginning of creating my leadership playlist and how I learned to hear the music again. Now, let's dive a little deeper into how music helps us stay focused and inspired.

MUSIC: THE UNTAPPED ADVANTAGE

"Music doesn't speak in particular words.
It speaks in emotions, and if it is in the bones, it's in the bones."
—*Keith Richards*

I am often asked, "Why music? Why is music an inspiration?"

Music is a universal language that transfers across all cultures, and when engaged properly, true transformation can happen. When you attach memories, motivations, thoughts, and actions to music, then the whole composition begins to be laid out in your mind as a melody does on a sheet of music. Your whole self begins to appear.

After I got my driver's license when I was 16 years old, my friends and I would spend Saturday afternoons at our local record store, Peaches, listening to music and purchasing more 45s than we knew what to do with. We would slide our way through narrow rows of vinyl two feet deep, looking for that one record we had spent the past week listening to, memorizing all the lyrics. The tips of my fingers should probably have calluses on them from all the filtering we did to find the record with that one perfect song.

Now, I turn it over to you with a question: What is one song you remember from your younger years? Are you thinking of the song and/or the memories that are attached to it?

As I mentioned earlier, we all have a soundtrack to our memories: Our first date, concerts and hanging at the pool, working in a hot restaurant, or driving with friends on a Sunday afternoon. Each memory likely has a song that comes to mind. When I was a senior in high school, I loved listening to Fleetwood Mac, The Cars, The Eagles, Van Morrison, and The Rolling Stones. Now, every time I hear one of those songs, the memories come flooding back—mostly with happiness or a life lesson.

I have many memories of my time with music and how it has shaped not only who I am but my business career as well. I am on the tail end of a phenomenal generation called the Baby Boomers. When I was young, I saw people expressing feelings openly with sit-ins, at Woodstock, or at war protests. But I also saw people who didn't speak at all, afraid to say the wrong thing at the wrong time, especially to friends and family. As for me, I pushed my feelings down into the pit of my belly.

Dyslexia impacted my thoughts, feelings, and choice of words, and when I wanted to speak or feel something of my own, I chose music to help me organize my thoughts in a way that made sense to me. I chose music because it understood me, and I understood it. I can put myself back into a song and recall those feelings and how music pushed me through both good and bad days during my teens.

In 1976, I was in middle school. It was a pivotal time in my life with lots of changes. The biggest change I was attempting to understand was why I thought it was important to switch from swimming, a sport I loved, to cheerleading, a sport all the girls in my school wanted to participate in. Swimming was such a massive part of my life that my coach had to tell me it was probably a better idea to sleep in my pajamas instead of my swimsuit! However, I decided to try out for cheerleading since all my friends were, and I thought it would be fun.

I wound up making the cheerleading squad and found myself cheering through my junior year in high school (that's another story for another book). However, I believe that's when life became new to me. As a swimmer, I was alone in the pool, pushing myself, talking in my head. I could see the competition out of the corner of my eye. I was comfortable in that space, and I was well on my way to the Junior Olympics.

Cheerleading was a brand-new experience. I was now a part of a team whose decisions were made collectively. I started to wear makeup and wanted to be pretty, and we all wore the same uniform. Most girls had their hair in a ponytail, and I had a head full of curls, so I stood out in a way I didn't want to.

Here is where music found me—again.

Cheerleading was a lot like music. We had cheers, movements, and even dance steps that we would practice daily to ensure we were all in sync, in harmony. When I finally came home, I would run to my room and start the vinyl, turning on my stereo. I listened to Billy Joel's album "The Stranger" for so long that I began to write and dream of a playscript and how it would be played out on stage with scenes from an Italian restaurant. Although I felt off tempo and wanted to be back in the pool, I knew the best thing to do was push through. So that's what I did.

Can you think of an experience when you were younger that you had to learn how to push yourself through? Did music help you, too?

A MODERN VIEW OF LEADERSHIP

> "Music is... a higher revelation than
> all Wisdom & Philosophy."
> —*Ludwig van Beethoven*

I often wonder if there is a time when we stop growing professionally. Is it when we think we've climbed the ladder and reached success? I don't believe so. Leaders are vigorous learners. We continuously soak up knowledge and skills. However, we often don't get the time to step aside from the hustle of everyday business to reflect on our choices and who we have become as a leader—or even as a person!

As leaders, we need to rise above the grind and explore the legacy we want to leave and how we will be remembered. This is when a leader shows up—when they are willing to serve their people and think about what happens after they leave.

When we look at the history of business and business leaders, we can see the evolution and innovation with new technologies and a new generation of leaders. Each generation, from the Baby Boomers to Gen Z, defines what leadership could look like from their perspectives. Those descriptions may stem from their defining world moments in life: the moon landing, Vietnam, the energy crisis, 9/11, Y2K, and more recently, the COVID-19 pandemic. These defining moments bring different perspectives into organizations and, therefore, into leadership expectations.

What people expect from their leaders keeps changing, and it is our responsibility to understand how to serve people best. However, I don't want to stop there. Your legacy is about the impact you have and the gift you leave when you are promoted, find a new job, or relocate to a new city. Every day is an opportunity to write your Authentic Leadership Legacy.

Today, as we are working from home for 18 months and counting, there is an overwhelming call for compassion, empathy, and understanding. While I believe this to be true, I also have over 30 years of experience in the corporate world. The sad truth is that all people—women *or* men—who demonstrate empathy, caring, or compassion can be labeled as weak, motherly, and even overly sensitive. These labels will eventually begin to separate you from the pack until you are standing alone on an island, wondering what happened. However, I want to tell you that the way you lead has little to do with what others think or how they label you.

It's OK not to fit the rigid mold of what the world thinks a leader *should* be. You are a much more effective leader when you lead with *your* unique skillset, and what we will discover later as your Side B Legacy Behavior. These are positive, emotion-based behaviors that live deep within us that we are often afraid to bring to the forefront of our leadership. This causes us to be unbalanced in leadership, similar to missing a piece in your band.

What would "Stairway to Heaven" by Led Zeppelin be without a guitar? It would most definitely be unbalanced, and a huge piece of its power and impact would be missing.

It's time to be you. It's time to forget about the titles and fame. It is far more important to do the work you stamp with *your* name.

Think about what the world would be like if you only led with tenacity, grit, discipline, accountability, and toughness. Now, think about what it would be like if you only led with compassion, empathy, understanding, and tenderness. Each of these scenarios would have its own problems to overcome, like an environment based strictly on fear or one based strictly on kindness. Balancing these behaviors is essential for the workplace. To have genuine strength and authenticity as a leader, understanding both sides of a coin—or in this book, both sides of a record—is valuable for the people you serve.

Can you hold someone accountable with kindness? Yes.

Can you expect results with discipline and understanding? Yes.

Can you serve an employee with toughness and tenderness? Yes, and it is the best thing you can do to serve your employees.

The key is to be who you truly are and show up in your Authentic Leadership Legacy, the behavior that shines with your whole self (ALL of you).

Will you earn your scars along the way as you're learning to show up as your whole self? Yes, that's inevitable. We all make mistakes. Instead of getting down about them, ask yourself, "What did I learn?" Don't sell yourself short. You are a unique leader, and that is special for the people you serve. So, remove the self-doubt and roadblocks standing in your way, and remember you are doing this for all the people you serve, not yourself.

WHEN YOUR WHOLE SELF SHOWS UP

Climbing the corporate ladder is what it takes to be successful. The path is already paved:

Go to school.

Go to college, if you are able.

Find a job.

Find a spouse.

Buy a house.

Settle down with kids.

Get promoted.

Retire.

Or, at least that's what I thought. Maybe you did, too.

When you were young, and the whole world seemed to be ahead of you, did you dream of being a CEO or VP of Sales? Probably not.

I wanted to be a lead singer in an all-girl band or a teacher. I had friends who wanted to be a dump truck driver, teacher, firefighter, nurse, doctor, or zookeeper. Now, take a moment and look through those for a second. All those dreams are about serving people and communities. However, as we journey through our teen years, we start to shift our dreams, and sometimes, we let money, parents, or other people's expectations define our journey or write our song. This is when I am reminded of the song "Everyday People" by Sly and the Family Stone.

When we finally choose a career path to follow, most of the time, we begin by laying out the necessary skills to advance our careers and the salary we need, and that becomes our main focus. As we do so, the dreamer in us who wanted to help people as a firefighter or nurse fades away, and often so does the desire to serve others.

The thing is, no matter what career path you choose, you can still bring your whole self to the "office." You don't have to leave some of what makes the best of you behind.

At the time of this writing, I am 57 years old. In hindsight, climbing the corporate ladder was a fantastic journey; it led me to helping people understand their goals, their gifts, and their motivations and inspirations. I was always under the impression that once you reach the top, you will be rewarded, so it's important to get there. But what is the reward? I have climbed a few ladders only to find I haven't reached the top that I envisioned in my heart.

Use Your Passions

Alternative School. Remember that back in the '80s? We all thought it was for students who couldn't "handle" high school. Looking back on it, they were actually the smart students! They were following their inspiration and getting ahead in their passions to find careers in their field. What a brilliant idea. Every student should be able to go forth with that sort of inspiration, not just waiting for the spring musical to highlight the on-stage talent. These students were given the opportunity to lean into their gifts and talents in a way that traditional schools did not, and I cannot imagine how fulfilling that must be to each of them.

Now, before we go any further, I have to confess that I cannot sing or play an instrument. Actually, I am so offbeat it's funny, so that career is out, right?

Or so I thought.

Yet once more, decades later, I am finding my inspiration again. Sometimes, you have to go back to when you were a kid and look at what you loved to do… then find a way to do it for a living. There were career paths in the music industry other than being a frontwoman or a recording artist, but no one talked about it. Trust me; I don't want to go back and start over. However, I do want to be inspired by what makes me happy, which is music.

I am amazed by my daughter, who helped me understand what it means to show up as your whole self. She is incredibly creative and willing to step out of the norm and take chances. She is now 27 years old and living a life she loves. However, that was not always the case.

When she was in high school, she auditioned for a performance group. She wasn't accepted and was told it was because I forgot to sign the release form. At the time, she was completely devastated. But that setback provided opportunities for change and new avenues to explore. Not long after, she was offered the opportunity to become a street team leader for a record label, which had her assisting in grassroots marketing for the label's artists coming to our hometown. Her job was to promote the band by creating signs or displaying "chalk" logos on the sidewalk.

She did this for several years, and through the experience, figured out what she wanted to do for a career. She went to college and continued to work for the record company during the summer, touring with a cross-country music festival that played in multiple cities for the duration of the summer. She sold merchandise; however, what she was really doing was building her network of professionals and getting her name out in the industry. She has grown brilliantly in her career, touring with established artists in arenas and continuing to pursue the life she has worked so hard to build.

Following your passion and uncovering your song is what it takes to bring your whole self to leadership, and that is why leadership is rewarding to me... if done right.

EXTRAORDINARY LEADERSHIP REQUIRES ALL OF YOU

As we navigate the never-ending changes in business, life, and personal growth, I wonder if we are missing out on the full conversation—a conversation that started within ourselves so long ago. The part of the conversation that allowed us to feel emotion.

I have always been inspired by lyrics, and early on, I began to notice the emotional pull they had on me when I was happy, sad, frustrated, or passionate. As I was listening to one of my favorite albums, "Legend: The Best of Bob Marley", I noticed that each song had its own emotion of happiness, sadness, frustration, or passion and thought, *Wow, people do, too!*

With our world becoming busier and busier, we are beginning to expect everything at a moment's notice, our emotions give way to problem-solving, and our leaders are on 24/7. I have seen this change in CEOs and senior leaders when they are promoted into that titled position, including myself.

It is in that change that we lose the feeling of what it was like when first starting our career. We tend to lose the emotions we feel when starting a new job, like being scared or nervous, wanting to do well and accomplish goals for our new leaders. As we begin to grow in our careers, we find it can be lonely in our office, and yet we don't recognize that part of us is missing. We experience over half of our waking time in the corporate world, but we don't spend enough time with people to help us find that positive emotional pull.

Are you ready to be a leader for the future, an extraordinary leader who taps into their whole self to embrace and attract people who want to be around them? It's time to balance your résumé skills and your people skills. It's time to turn up the music and find the melody *and* accompanying harmony in your business self.

It's time to uncover your Side B Behavior.

SIDE B

RCA introduced the 45 as a way to put a hit song on one side of that little vinyl record. The most common form of the vinyl single is the 45 (named because of its play speed of 45 rpms) or 7-inch (it was 7 inches in diameter). Of course, they couldn't leave the other side blank, so there was always a song on side B that was kind of like a younger, less glamorous sibling… or the "unpopular" alter ego of side A.

Side B is the lesser-known side; the side we don't often play. It doesn't get a lot of recognition, but given a chance, it's probably a hit. If we think about it, maybe it was an opportunity for a band to get creative and play with different sounds and musical choices. It was always a bit of a risk to play something off-brand; however, sometimes, it showed who the band truly was as artists.

At the time, Side B was not a high-stakes song. Have you heard of KISS, a hardcore, heavy-metal rock band from the mid-'70s? If not, you gotta check them out. Anyway, they recorded a Side B song called "Beth". It was a piano ballad, which wasn't their brand... AT ALL. This song was going to be the "silent track" to the big hit "Detroit Rock City".

Wrong.

"Beth" became the biggest hit for KISS and the only one that got significant airplay. Here are a few more Side B songs you might recognize: "Hound Dog" by Elvis; "Good Riddance" by Green Day; "I Am the Walrus" by The Beatles; "Maggie May" by Rod Stewart; "Can't Always Get What You Want" by The Rolling Stones, and "(We're Gonna) Rock Around The Clock" by Bill Haley & His Comets. These are all Side B songs that people fell into and fell in love with. Weren't we lucky to hear those being played on the radio?

And wouldn't the world be lucky to hear *your* Side B? Wouldn't the world be a better place? Wouldn't the company be extraordinary? Wouldn't the employee and customer experience be extraordinary? Wouldn't retention be extraordinary?

Yes, Side B was added to support Side A, the popular money maker and the "make it big" song; but without Side B, those songs may have never hit the stores in my time.

I used to line up at the record store with my friends to get that newly released song by an artist playing on the radio. Very rarely did I look at the second song, Side B, because, in my mind, there was no possible way that song could be a better recording. Right? It was there for good measure, for support, as the producers didn't want to take away from the newly released song.

However, what I found out later was the artist often put something off-brand or a song that was quickly pulled together for Side B, and it usually came together at the last possible moment.

Those last-minute songs usually came quickly from the heart, soul, and mind of the artists without much thought or practice, as it was "only going to be the Side B." Therefore, there was no need to spend much time on the song, and it came about organically—and *fast*. If that creativity did not occur, we might not have landed on Side B brilliance. By the way, "Wipe Out" by The Surferies was a Side B release as well, never intended to make a splash in music.

Side B in Leadership

So, what does all this have to do with leadership?

Let's think of leadership as a record album with two sides. Side A has all your résumé skills, competencies, and traits (i.e., communication skills, work ethic, or being tech-savvy), while Side B reflects your behaviors and traits related to emotion— ones we don't talk about often, like curiosity, trustworthiness, and passion. Listening and learning from each side

AUTHENTIC LEADERSHIP LEGACY

will allow your Authentic Leadership Legacy to flourish, and your teams to reach goals you only dreamed of.

What if I told you that Side B is your greatest strength in leadership? Wouldn't you want to explore, strengthen, or even hone those characteristics to bring out the best in yourself, your employees, and your company?

As I began to take note of the similarities between leadership behaviors and Side B songs, I also began to understand that Side B is where I wanted to be. It was also important to me to *write* from this track—Side B, the silent track of leadership. I realized that passion, trustworthiness, courage, and kindness were my strengths, and that's when it changed. That's when *I* changed.

WHAT ABOUT MUSIC?

Think about it: We hear music in the car, stores, malls, coffee shops, movies, TV theme songs, and commercials. We even hear it in the surrounding of nature, the crackling of fire, the chirping of birds, and the chatterbox in our heads. So, why not music in leadership development?

This is your journey, and you have the power to choose your lyrics, your tempo, your rhythm—your song. It's time for others to hear your Side B song loud and clear, and I humbly ask that you take this journey with me and enjoy the ride into the fusion of music and leadership. As leaders, we often seek new ways of growing our skills, competencies, and career, but how often do we try to grow in our character? I believe we can do that through music, and that, my friend, is the ultimate leadership hack.

LIVING YOUR LEGACY BEHAVIOR

How will you be remembered? Do you know? If you do know, are you satisfied with the answer?

It is not up to you to "create" a legacy; however, you *do* have the opportunity to choose a direction and the work you will do to live a life worth remembering. This involves inner work and self-awareness that brings forth those parts of you that will help define your legacy using both Side A and Side B behaviors.

Now, I know how hard you are working. Most senior leaders are workaholics focused on building the business and achieving results and thus lose sight of their "people" gift. What I mean by "people gift" is simply another way to express your Side B behaviors that are left silent. Ultimately, as that gift goes unnoticed by the people you serve, so does the memory that gift would create.

So, I ask you again: How are you showing up today, and what legacy are you leading for the people you serve?

There are plenty of ways in which the word "legacy" is used, according to dictionaries. Money or property left to you in a will by someone who has passed; something that is a part of your history; a situation that has left a mark on your past, or a product that has been so widely used it is no longer available.

Legacy is not simply one thing; it is not just the obituary written about you after you are gone. Legacy is your family, the stories told during get-togethers, achievements accomplished at both home and work. It is also the emotional impact you leave on a group of people when you hit your highest revenue goals, leave a department you were promoted from, or the legacy left when you retire. Much like your favorite band, you don't know all their accomplishments, but you do know how their songs made you *feel*. In this book, we will refer to legacy as the part of you seen by others in any career move. This is the way you treat people that you associate with and serve, how you show up each workday, and how you use your natural gifts to influence others.

It is important to discover and uncover who we are as we serve people and help write the future for the generations of upcoming leaders. We must prepare to leave the team, people, and company in the best shape possible. This book is not about making a name for yourself or the title you hold; it is about the silent serving of people. It will ultimately be the people you leave behind who describe your legacy, not you. You do, however, hold the power to utilize your Side B—the best part of you—and leave the legacy you desire to leave. Yes, your legacy is a gift to others, and you can choose to make it a positive or negative one.

But, if legacy is something willed or left behind, then who is it left to? Your peers, your teammates, your department, the people you serve? Or maybe it's all of them. Remember, at each step of your progression in your career, you are leaving something behind, and with each person you interact with, you leave your legacy.

Flip the Organizational Chart

As a young manager, there was a time when I was leading a team of six individuals. They were a phenomenal team! Everything a manager could want, really. However, I was not a great leader, and I was trying to be everything I thought my leaders wanted me to be. So, I watched the team like a hawk. My name was Mrs. Micro-Manager, a name I earned and did not want. I made the results, the team, and actions all about me. I wanted to be the best, and the best, in my eyes, was managing everyone and everything.

When I finally woke up nine months later, everyone was gone. They left for a better leader; I literally drove them away. You know that feeling in the pit of your stomach, that "What did I do, how do I make this better" kind of feeling? I definitely felt that. Obviously, the results plummeted, and I, in turn, learned that there were some changes I needed to make immediately and internally to be a better leader.

This was when I started looking for help to learn the "secret leadership language." Nothing really resonated with me, so I decided to broaden my scope, and it led to me attending an executive retreat. I went for education on best practices for building and growing a sales team, but what I walked away with was much more valuable. The keynote speaker was Duane Cummings, an entrepreneur, coach, consultant, and someone who would become a very dear friend. Duane was speaking about a leadership mindset. During his presentation, I heard four simple words that got the gears in my mind working: "Flip the organizational chart."

Wait, what?! I was always told to work for your boss. I was taught that your job is to do everything you can to make your boss look good. So, what was this crazy idea?

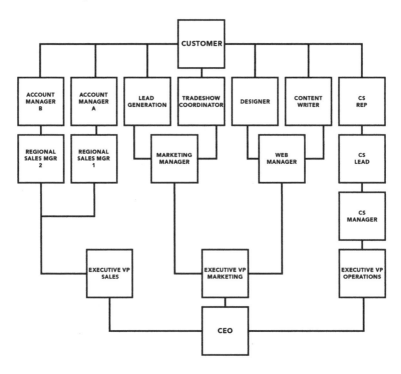

Eventually, as I thought long and hard about it, that idea became more real. Here is what that phrase means: Your job is to serve your team, who, in turn, will serve the customer. When you serve the customer, your team is achieving results, you are growing the business and now serving your leaders' objectives, and so on... like a bow sliding up and down the strings of a violin that makes beautiful music. This quite beautifully sums up what an extraordinary leader does daily: They work for the team.

On my flight home, it became evident what I needed to do as a leader. The plan was in place, and now it was time to believe and execute the plan. Listen, not only did I flip the organizational chart, but I also shook up the culture. The entire attitude of our office and the motivation of our team changed exponentially. It was a "team-first/self-last" motto.

What amazed me was what hiring a mentor and four simple words could do for my self-esteem, vision, and beliefs. This can happen for you, as well, when you invest in yourself.

From that moment on, that is how I led teams. *I work for you; you work for the customer.* It was discussed in every interview that reached my desk and executed daily with the team. Sure, I had my fair share of bad days where I didn't stay focused on this motto, we all do, but it was always my overarching theme.

Let's Work Together

So, what will your legacy be? I have identified 10 emotion-based Legacy Behaviors, which you will learn more about later in the book. These Legacy Behaviors are often unseen in leadership, and if you keep an open mind, you will see that walking in your personal Legacy Behavior will have a compound effect on your company. People will be lining up to work with you, and they will trust you. Let me say that again: There will be *trust* within the organization.

Defining your legacy is not for you; it's for the people you lead. They deserve the opportunity to build their career with positive influences. If you understand it is with the people you serve that your legacy will be defined, you are well on your way to leaving a great legacy.

Song: "Let's Work Together"
Let's work together
There's nothing that we cannot do
Let's work together
Believe me, I believe in you

Lyrics by Paula White

CHAPTER 2

THE POWER OF MUSIC
(AND LEADERSHIP)

"Music gives a soul to the universe,
wings to the mind, flight to the imagination,
and life to everything"
—*Plato*

Henry is waiting in the doctor's office to be seen for his headaches that have been rapidly increasing. He is working from his phone and answering texts back and forth, impatiently waiting for the nurse to call him back. Every so often, he looks up from the phone when the door to the "other side" opens. It is still not his turn, so back to his phone he goes, answering emails and feeling an urgent need to get back to the office—quickly.

Henry then notices it is very quiet in the lobby, and he can hear the dripping of the water tank across the room. Drip,

drip, drip, every two to three seconds. The louder and louder it becomes, he wonders in the back of his mind if anyone else notices the sound. Now only able to focus on the water dripping, he desperately wants to get up and fix it.

Suddenly, the door flies open, and his name is called. *Whew!* Henry finally gets to walk back to an examination room, knowing in his head that he is either looking at the screen too much or he is anxious because the company is falling just short of their goal and the board meeting is in a few weeks.

As he is waiting for the doctor, music starts playing over the speakers in the room. It's "Blackbird" by the Beatles. Henry sits back, lets his mind wander, and takes a journey down memory lane. He begins to remember the first car he bought for himself when he turned 16. This was the song playing when he first passed his driver's test and could drive solo. He named his car Blackbird; it helped that it was a black Datsun 210.

WIRED FOR MUSIC

I wonder if Henry knows he is at the beginning of his next journey, the next season of his life. He is beginning to notice the small sounds around him, and while some are irritating, like the steady dripping of water, others bring back memories of happiness.

Music is a part of our everyday life. You hear, feel, and experience it in just about every situation you can think of: at a restaurant, in a lobby, in your car, during commercials, at stores, casinos, movies, and in television shows. However, maybe you can relate with me here—at a certain point in my life, I noticed that the older I became, the more I began to tune music out. I tuned out the music I once listened to on a hot summer's day or while getting ready for work. Instead, I began listening to podcasts, talk shows, and maybe a baseball game on the radio with my husband. I wouldn't recommend that, however; baseball games on the radio are not entertaining, at least to me!

It wasn't until I was driving home from work late one night by myself that something changed. I started to scan the stations and heard "Fly Like an Eagle" by the Steve Miller Band. I began to let down my guard and sing at the top of my lungs. I mean, no one could see or hear me as I was in the car... right? After the song was done, those fateful words came through the program host: "Thank you for listening to Classic Rock 107.9!" I burst out laughing in my car, thinking, *I am old. I AM OLD!*

Whether old or young, what I do know is that music is one of the most beautiful ways to bring clarity and creativity to our world, and as we get busy with living our adult life, we have lost the time to enjoy and explore new music along the way.

According to Daniel J. Levitin, Ph.D. and *New York Times* Best Seller, the mind refers to the part of us that embodies thoughts, desires, memories, beliefs, and experiences. The brain, on the other hand, is an organ or collection of cells.[1]

Now, think about this distinction for a moment when it comes to music. A musical composition would be the brain,

---

[1] Daniel J. Levitin "This is Your Brain on Music" Chapter 3, Behind the Curtain Pg. 83

holding all the notes and lyrics. The mind, on the other hand, holds the melody we'd like to express in the form of our feelings, experiences, and beliefs. Using both our mind and brain together, we can listen to and comprehend the sound.

We have come to understand through many past studies that music impacts the whole brain, not just the right or left side. This fact makes music enormously powerful and unique, as it is rare to come across a medium that uses the whole brain. However, music affords us that very opportunity. As leaders, having the capability to tap into our whole brain gives us the power to bring our whole selves into our role. That, in and of itself, is one reason why music is enormously powerful.

How might music play a part in our lives as leaders, and can it even begin, in the simplest of terms, to affect change for ourselves?

Is music transformational? Does music have the power to change our emotions and personality?

The article "Plato on Music" from the website *Popular Beethoven* speaks to Plato's thoughts about the power that music holds over our body and soul:

> According to Plato, music is able to bypass reason and penetrate the very core of the self, causing great impact on the character: "because more than anything else, rhythm and harmony find their way into the inmost soul and take the strongest hold upon it."[2]

---

[2] https://www.popularbeethoven.com/plato-on-music/

In addition to the power music holds when it comes to our physical and emotional being, another interesting point of note is that often, the importance of music increases in adolescence into early adulthood and decreases again until retirement.

I found this conclusion to be very interesting and began to ask myself a few simple questions. Why does it decrease during our adult years? Could it be because we are so focused on building our career and family that we simply have other priorities? Or could it be that we don't see the benefit that music offers when it comes to the workplace? The answers are worth pondering, but I will leave that to the professionals. I am positive, however, that music is emotional at its core, and emotions are what drive us to believe in what we are doing while building a strong foundation for serving others.

MUSIC IN THE WORKPLACE

We use MS Word for writing brilliant thoughts, Salesforce for marketing automation, Post-it Notes for creative sessions, and the classic suggestion jar to gather ideas from the team. We employ many tools to get the job done, advance in our careers, and manage teams, so why not music?

Joshua Leeds, author of *The Power of Sound,* brings out two interesting discoveries about music as it relates to the corporate world, the first being this: In 1995, The University of Illinois studied 256 office workers and found that those who listened to their music of choice on headphones increased simple clerical work performance by 14% and more complex work by 7%.[3]

If music increases performance or productivity, why do corporate office buildings only stream "white noise" with the purpose of decreasing the background office sounds of people talking on the phone? (If they stream anything at all!) Perhaps you have been in a corporate office and heard "white noise" streaming. It probably sounded like you were flying in an airplane at 30,000 feet and sitting next to the wing. It was a mere humming noise to keep other sounds quiet.

Now "white noise," as we call it, is most commonly heard in office buildings, baby sleep machines, and airplanes. However, there are many other "colors" of noise. Some of the most popular colors of noise include white, pink, brown, and blue, each with its own frequency. These are often used for the same purposes as white noise, namely, to invoke feelings of peace or ease or drown out other noise. However, it is important to understand that each person reacts differently to each of these frequencies. Therefore, we shouldn't assume one sound fits all. I see this fact as supporting my belief that music is emotional to everyone, just like your leadership style is unique to you.

Leeds also shared, "For some executives, making music is just as important as making money. [Whether it is] Opera,

[3] https://www.washingtonpost.com/archive/lifestyle/wellness/1995/10/24/music-via-headphone-may-boost-job-performance/fee1883d-99b6-44db-a727-a1295e5eb66c/

Rock, Cabaret, or Country, music represents for them the ultimate escape from the rigors of corporate life."[4]

I relate well to this comment, as listening to the radio or a Spotify playlist on my drive home from work allows me time to wind down and reflect on the day. I use the time to ask myself what I missed or generate a new idea to increase sales. It took me most of my 30-year corporate career to understand what a 30-minute drive home while listening to music could do for my health *and* business!

With my experience in mind, don't be afraid to let your inner musician sing on the way home from work. You don't need tinted windows or soundproof glass; instead, just let it flow and get your groove on to whatever song helps you decompress or motivate yourself!

Circling back to Plato, if you believe that his beliefs are accurate and music *can* imitate emotions, then let's consider the empowerment of music in leadership and all the good it can bring to self-awareness and discovery. To better understand and display our Side B Legacy Behaviors, I believe there are three areas of music for us to focus on: musical memory, musical motivation, and musical mindset.

MUSICAL MEMORY

To be fully transparent and honest, the concept of musical memory is what helped me get through school having

---

[4] Joshua Leeds, *Power of Sound*

dyslexia. Yes, it was challenging at first. I thought I was slow at reading, unfocused, and unable to keep up with others; however, my parents explained that my brain worked differently than others'. They helped me understand that this difference didn't make me weak; rather, it made me unique.

From that point on, I knew what I had to do to succeed. I had to push myself like I did in the pool. I found that when listening to the radio, I was better at memorizing words, ideas, and thoughts. Therefore, I began to use that rhythmic beat to help me memorize better. Music helped me with tests and to knock down any obstacles that hindered me in school. I found my brain would think twice as fast as the words that came from my mouth, which would confuse the people around me. Fortunately, I had some teachers, like Mr. Phillips, for example, that would sit me down and wait until I could collect my thoughts and put them together. That patience was vital to my success in school and now in business.

To help myself in school, I started to think of the words coming from my mouth as a song. For example, when taking a test on the human anatomy, I would simply put the words to a song that would fit the bones: skull, hyoid, vertebrae, ribs, and sternum… all the way down the skeletal system. I would also use music as a tool to remember important historical events and facts. For example, I once put the Gettysburg Address to music.

Today, we are learning more than ever before about how to teach people with dyslexia to shape their thoughts and excel. For me, I only knew it as a "reading problem" until my grandfather, who was also dyslexic, told me that I could accomplish anything because no one could push me harder than I would push myself.

In business, being dyslexic is my strength, even my superpower! Yet, I tried to hide it from so many. What I didn't realize until just recently was that being dyslexic has made me a strong leader and a strong woman. I was able to think differently than others and look at business from a unique perspective. However, I was having trouble expressing it in a way that leaders could understand. Patience is not really a trademark in leadership, and I didn't want to be seen as weak or unfocused. There were a few leaders and peers who truly knew me and understood that my thoughts worked faster than my speaking. Therefore, they would let me talk until my words finally caught up with my brain. That, to me, demonstrated true leadership, and I thank them for that!

As a business leader, my environment was different than school; I didn't have tests or quizzes to remember. However, I was responsible for presenting business plans and concepts to leaders, and with each promotion, I presented to a new set of people that didn't necessarily understand how I thought, and I had to remind myself that being dyslexic is okay. I would prepare presentations with ideas to grow our department and use quotes and words from industry experts to help get my points across.

Unfortunately, there was not always enough time for the presentation, and sometimes I was asked to turn the presentation over to the leaders. At one point, I was even told that anyone can use other people's words in a presentation, but that doesn't make it a "plan." In response, I simply asked, "May I walk you through it?" During the conversation that followed, I spoke with clarity using my "learned" techniques to slow my thoughts down and my slides as a composition to put my brain into a rhythm.

Dyslexia is often thought of as only mixing up words and numbers; however, it is so much more. It has auditory, sensory, and anxiety components that are complex. That is why music is a fascinating tool for memory; when music is playing in my mind, I am much more focused, clear, and creative. I become driven to execute tasks and passionate to help others. Therefore, as an extraordinary leader, I remind you that up to 10%-20% of the population (according to the International Dyslexia Association, the Dyslexia Center of Utah, and many other resources) has dyslexia. Having someone with dyslexia on your team is a gift. Once you give them the opportunity to be a part of your organization, make time to slow down and listen.

The Power of Nostalgia

Musical memories bring us back to a place of nostalgia, and more importantly, a time when we were open to learning and growing. Even those who are not lovers of music will still find their everyday lives impacted by it.

As a senior in high school, I loved listening to Fleetwood Mac, The Cars, The Eagles, Boston, David Bowie, Michael Jackson, Jackson Browne, Bob Marley, and Anita Baker—again, you name the band, I listened to it. Although back then, you were supposed to be either a fan of The Beatles or The Rolling Stones—but not both. It was the whole "which one was the most popular British band" thing. However, I liked them both.

All these bands would regularly be a part of Casey Kasem's *American Top 40*, a radio show airing from 1970-1988 which counted down the Billboard Top 40 Hits for the week. Casey Kasem was a successful disc jockey, radio personality, and voiceover actor. In the late '70s, he also hosted a live Friday night song request show where listeners would write in and request a song for that special someone. My friends and I would listen for hours on the off chance that one of our names would be heard. (Mind you, this was across America, so the chances were slim.)

The part that was the most fun was listening with a group of people on Friday nights when there wasn't a football or basketball game to go to. When I think about it now, my mind goes right back to playing pool, cards, or just talking with a great group of friends.

This nostalgia is why I often ask the leaders I work with to share with me three songs from their childhood, their high school years, and their present. About 90% of my clients come back with incredibly happy songs from their childhood, then a pattern of intense, emotionally driven songs (mostly about love) during high school, ending with songs that elicit strong positive or negative emotions.

Now, I am not a psychologist, and therefore I don't have the answers as to why our teen years appear to be a time for more intense songs and lyrics (that seem to drive a lot of conversations about uncomfortable topics). However, what I will say is that if you can reframe some of those negative memories and find the songs that you *did* enjoy, it will help you shape those memories so you can let go of that clutter in your brain and make way for productivity and positivity.

How Beats in Music Make Messages Stick

Musicians use a metronome to keep tempo while playing or creating music; I imagine mostly because it's hard to stay on time (and I'd go as far as to say that many of us are naturally out of rhythm). Tempo, meaning the song's speed, is calculated by beats per minute (BPM). Staying on time at a particular BPM allows the listener to hear the music in an organized structure and tap their feet, clap their hands, or memorize the lyrics.

Now, I'm not ashamed to admit that I still sing the ABCs in my head to remember what comes after the letters J or P. (I'll bet you're secretly shaking your head and saying, "Me too!") I would also wager that most of us are tired of singing the "The Hokey Pokey". However, love it or hate it, this classic wedding song has a specific tempo that helps us remember its melody and lyrics.

While remembering the ABCs or the Hokey Pokey song is not executive in nature, you may find it interesting to learn that the number of beats per minute a song has affects each person differently. Given this fact, it's important to know which BPM will personally motivate you. A good starting point may be 80-115 beats per minute, as memorable workout songs usually land within that range.

Let's reframe how beats may help you as a leader. Leaders need uninterrupted time for better focus and productivity. Just like those songs from our younger years, our memories become attuned to beats that bring us into a certain state of being. For example, I listened to a YouTube channel called *Good Vibes – Binaural Beats* and was able to choose the music that was best suited for me to write this book. However, that same choice would not be my "get me up and go" song. Instead, my choice there would be "Bright Side of the Road" by Van Morrison.

I personally think of musical beats as my heartbeat, keeping that constant pulse on my mind, brain, and moods. I could be having a terribly bad day, unfocused and stalled, but when I turn on Van Morrison, I become extremely focused. Do you know your "one song," that song that will change your mood instantaneously, the one you remember with positive memories? If you want to take it a step further, knowing what tempo ranges you relate to best could help you find music to increase your productivity, and even go from frustrated to calm at a moment's notice.

Messages as Music

Let me throw a "what if" question to you as a leader. What if you thought of yourself as a songwriter and started your year with an important message or theme for your team to drive results? And what if I told you that message could be remembered simply because of the way it was delivered at that one moment in time? What would it look like if your team remembered the significance of a single moment in a message you delivered? This means your message would have its own tempo, timing, and melody, not just lyrics. Your message would even have its own return on investment, or ROI.

What if?

I remember one such meeting. It was October 19, and I was in Park City, Utah, for another leadership retreat. It was the last day of the event, and we were waiting for the final speaker in the main room. I was sitting towards the front of the room, not wanting to be there, thinking I could just go to the airport early and grab a bite to eat without missing anything. This message was written all over my face and body language. Those who know me certainly know I don't have a poker face; most people can read my emotions from a mile away.

The leader started with a question: "How hot is it in here?" (The air conditioner was on, so that was unexpected.) She just stood still for a moment and went on to configure her speech like a song with a repeatable chorus, a bridge, and a few verses. I was fully engaged and laughing the whole time. And I sure am glad I did not miss her keynote after all.

The power was in her delivery—the song structure, if you will—and her tone of voice. She kept her main point (the chorus) in a lower or higher pitch than the rest of the speech (the song) so it would not get lost. It was incredible.

How does musical memory help us as leaders?

1. In times of crisis: Immediate recall for positive action.

2. In times of preparation: Training. Implement a plan using music to learn or recall an important skill or methodology. For example, the Bee Gees' song "Stayin' Alive" is about 100 BPM, the same rate recommended by the American Heart Association for "hands-only" CPR, was used in a campaign to help educate CPR learners on the proper tempo for chest compressions.

3. In times of growth: Write your presentations like a song!

4. In times of celebration: Energize. Kick off your meeting with music.

As a leader, if you can create a space in which your words are presented as a song, you boost your chances that everyone in the room will remember it—much like the first time you heard your favorite song.

MUSICAL MOTIVATION

Leaders must fill the essential role of motivating their teams. So, is it possible to use *music* for motivation? **Yes, motivation is emotion, and leadership is inspiration.**

"Motivational," "inspirational," and "extraordinary" are words that should define your leadership to those you serve. If you exhibit motivation and inspiration, employees, peers, and other people will naturally work with you. There is a craving among young professionals to know their leaders and be inspired by them. That is our role! Music helps us maintain that energy to unite, collaborate, communicate, and encourage that YES! feeling we all get when we are inspired. As a leader striving for outstanding results and achievement, it may be time to focus on motivating and inspiring the people we serve.

Music Unites

Athletics, stores, and entertainment all use music to motivate people, fans, and customers. When asked if leaders can use music to motivate, I have a simple, one-word answer: *Rocky*.

Honestly, who doesn't think of running up the steps of the Philadelphia Museum of Art when you hear that music? (If you don't know the song, it is "Gonna Fly Now" by Bill Conti.) It has an impressionable start with a build that inevitably gives people goosebumps. Pretty soon, your feet start tapping, and you want to jump up and conquer the day. It is a hero's song! Other songs that fit this category might be Rachel Platten's "Fight Song" or Queen's "We Will Rock You"—which incidentally, in 1977, was the Side B song to "We are the Champions"!

What these songs do is rally people together to focus on the same goal.

Positive vs. Negative Motivation

Imagine yourself in a cage deep within the ocean, getting ready to do a little shark-feeding excursion. You have your wetsuit, flippers, mask, tank, and breathing apparatus all working together. From the top of the cage, the team tosses in chum to encourage the sharks to circle. What is playing in your head? The two notes from *Jaws* or the non-distinctive voice from your "Calm" app?

"Hello Paula, everything is going to be okay. Please pause and take a deep breath in… and out…" (That deep breath was good for you, wasn't it?!)

Either way, the mood is set.

There is a big difference between positive and negative motivation. Simply stated, positive motivation inspires, while negative motivation stops people in their tracks—much like the *Jaws* music noted above. As extraordinary leaders, we all strive to achieve our goals, and the pressures can be intense. My question to you is this: Are you motivating and inspiring your team to a positive success, or are you negatively pushing and demanding results from your teams? Here's the difference: In the cage with the sharks, how are you reacting? Does your team resent you and leave early on June 30, the last day of the month and quarter? Or do you order pizza in because everyone is willing to stay and push for you, their leader, and the company?

We understand that pressure, either positive or negative, for results, sales, and efficiencies are much like a roller-coaster of intensity during the month, quarter, or year. I equate it to a great musical ballad. Think about it this way: The month starts like the prelude to "Bohemian Rhapsody" by Queen. Your company needs to achieve a goal, and as a great leader, you give space and time for your team to reach the results. However, as the deadlines approach for monthly, quarterly, or yearly goals, the song intensity picks up, and everyone is pushing to the finish. The deadline day has come and gone, and the song winds down, only to start again in just a few days. Highly intuitive sales leaders, who understand this trend, will work to positively impact results with an intentional mindset to motivate their teams.

So, instead of the "Bohemian Rhapsody" roller-coaster of motivation that we think of during the month of selling, what if you used a different sort of musical motivation to set the pace in a team meeting, boardroom, or presentation?

Here's my challenge. The next time you need to motivate your team, or you are looking to brainstorm new ideas, open your session with music. You will open the door to creativity and invite magic to happen. However, as the leader, you cannot be shy and must embrace the lyric, beat, or tone. Take out a shaker and burst into song! Walls will fall down, and you'll have raw talent ready to be harnessed.

If that is too much to start with, I want you to simply go around the room and ask each person what their favorite song is or the first concert they attended and watch how quickly the room opens up to communication, collaboration, and creativity.

Communication

Much like the songs of our high school years, music gives us the ability to communicate what we feel but may not be able to freely express. Now, I want you to apply that idea to leadership. It is the beginning of your fiscal year, and it is time to create a vision for the upcoming objectives, plans, and goals for your company. It is time to inspire and empower your team to share in this vision and create a positive impact. Sometimes, you might not have the right words to say; in that case, one way to express them could be to pick out a theme song for the year and play it often to rally the team when needed. You would have plenty of options to use this theme song throughout the year. You could quote the lyrics, email the song via YouTube, or simply play it at the beginning of an important meeting.

While this may sound a bit far-fetched, what I will remind you of is that people want to feel important and empowered by their leaders and employers. Many frontline people are tired and exhausted from their rigid day-to-day experiences. A leadership team should give them something they can listen to when they need to be uplifted for the day!

I tried this once in a team meeting, and it helped inspire 15 people to hit and exceed our quarterly sales goals. We were ending a three-day national sales meeting, and I was the only thing standing between the team and the door to freedom. Everyone was completely exhausted, poised in their seats, looking longingly towards the door. However, it was my responsibility to go over our plan of action and get the team excited about our new year. So, I broke out my speakers and blasted "Can't Stop the Feeling!" by Justin Timberlake (which was the fastest upbeat song I could think of at the time!) and asked the team to get up and move around. They reluctantly agreed, and then the power of music and movement took over. People started laughing, grinning, and leaving the decorum of work in favor of shared fun—the place where we learn and work together best.

By doing this, the team got focused, listened, and participated, and we were done 20 minutes early with an agreement to our game plan. They were accountable and delivered on the results.

I encourage you, don't forget to expand your view. And don't become stale. Loosen up a little!

The Yes! Factor

Researchers have been studying the reaction that music has on the brain, as well as our dopamine, serotonin, or endorphin levels, for years. These happy chemicals help our motivation and give us the feeling that anything can be accomplished.

According to a study done by Solomon H. Snyder at the Johns Hopkins University School of Medicine, dopamine modulates the reward experiences elicited by music for a lot of people. Lauren Ferreri, author of the study, has character- ized these findings as a first. She writes the following: "This study shows for the first time the causal role of dopamine in musical pleasure and motivation: enjoying a piece of music, deriving pleasure from it, wanting to listen to it again, being willing to spend money for it, strongly depend on the dopa- mine released in our synapses."[5]

---

[5] "Dopamine modulates the reward experiences elicited by music" PNAS February 26, 2019 116 (9) 3793-3798; first published January 22, 2019; https://doi.org/10.1073/pnas.1811878116

When you are happy, you are motivated to get started, implement, or finish that one task or project. This is dopamine in action. As leaders, we are more effective, productive, and happy when we are motivated. Seeking results and success, whatever that success may be to you, is that natural "YES!" feeling we strive for consistently. It's analogous to competitive swimmers holding their breath to reach the "T" at the end of the black line on the pool floor or musicians running on stage in front of the fans, ready to perform.

However, in addition to their uses in everyday life, we also need the ability to sense when something is wrong so we can be fully aware of any threats, obstacles, and warnings. This is the role of cortisol. Cortisol is less like a piece of music that you relate to and more like a song you gravitate towards on a bad day at work. Its messages are necessary to protect you or offer you a course correction. Think of it as your brain setting off an alarm that your plan is not working. Therefore, it is important to understand how music can affect your dopamine or cortisol levels and moods; find the music within yourself that lifts you and gets you moving, and then listen for those warning signals.

How does musical motivation help us as leaders?

1. In times of crisis: The surge of dopamine to complete a task.

2. In times of preparation: Music to energize and focus.

3. In times of growth: To motivate a team.

4. In times of celebration: Celebratory songs to reward your team.

MUSICAL MINDSET

Why do we sing in the shower, turn the music up in the car, or dance as we clean? Is it because we love to listen to music,

 or is it all a reaction to the natural increase in dopamine? Certainly, dopamine gives you the YES! feeling and energizes your mindset. However, it is incredibly important to be intentional with your choices and experiences to influence your decisions and empower the people you serve. It is up to *you* to decide what music is playing in your head. We all have a noisy critic, a chatterbox of sorts, and it is in a continuous fight with your ego.

Creativity and Being Intentional

Being intentional about the music you listen to on your way to and from work can help get you in the proper mindset to start and end your day well. However, there is another benefit and use for music, perhaps even more important than the first.

If you understand your triggers or find yourself stuck in a mindset of anger, frustration, or procrastination, that is precisely when you hit play on "that one song" to immediately course-correct and adjust your mindset. Granted, you must know what that song is and be very intentional about having it quickly at your fingertips!

For me, in this season of entrepreneurship, wanting to help people see the magic music can play in leadership, creativity, and results, it is "Those Conga Drums" by Jonathan Richman and The Modern Lovers. When I hit a roadblock, I just put it on and start to tap my feet, do a little chair dance, and increase that dopamine and serotonin!

As we get older, our seasons change along with our needs, our goals, and our surroundings. Therefore, our song does as well. In high school, my go-to song was "Landslide" by Fleetwood Mac. Still to this day, my friend Rachel and I light a candle to bring us back to that moment in time, which gives us a reminder that we can accomplish anything we put our minds to and will be there for each other, no matter the distance or length of time that has passed. Every time I hear this song, I am transported back to that moment in time with a grin on my face.

Now, you may already have a song like this. Or, as you start to listen more intently, you will know when you hear a song that encourages you to adjust your mood. However, you must be open to actively listening; a skill discussed more in detail later.

During a conversation with Lori Richardson, CEO and Entrepreneur of Score More Sales and Women Sales Pros, she shared that her favorite song is "The Climb" by Miley Cyrus. This song inspires Lori to act on her passion for seeing more women in the sales arena and empowers her to keep raising the level of awareness for it. She supports her cause with fresh data, energizing women to have a career in sales and encouraging male advocates to hire more women sales leaders. Lori encourages us to see the world beyond one generation, race, sex, or, as I would say, beyond one musical genre!

I recently had the remarkable opportunity to speak with David M. Greenberg, Ph.D. He is a psychologist, musician, and researcher at Bar-Ilan University and Cambridge University. His research examines music at the intersection of social science, neuroscience, genetics, and clinical treatment. I stumbled across one of his websites, Musical Universe. Here, you can take an assessment to uncover your musical preferences and personality—based on the Big Five Personalities—to help you understand how your brain works with music. You either operate with the Empathetic Brain, which has greater interest in emotions, or the Systemizing Brain, which has a greater interest in systems (or you might land somewhere in the middle).

Dr. Greenberg has studied music as a personality predictor backed by science and based on over 15 years of theory and research in cognitive neuroscience, social psychology, and personality science. Dr. Greenberg led a scientific study with a research team that included Jason Rentfrow, Michal Kosinski, and Daniel Levitin, that found that your personality has a bigger impact on the type of music you like than any other factor.

Similarly, Katherine Conrad writes the following in her article "Can Your Personality Explain Your iTunes Playlist?":

Turning to Facebook, the researchers recruited 9,500 participants to rate their personalities and musical preferences.

The group listened to 50 unfamiliar musical excerpts representing different levels of arousal, valence, and depth, and rated their preferences. They also took a standard personality test. The results revealed that neurotic individuals preferred music with negative emotions and intensity; open-minded and liberal people liked complex melodies, while those who identified as agreeable and extroverted liked songs with positive emotions.[6]

If our musical tastes are linked to our personalities, which, according to the study, is a stronger link than previously thought, and music affects us emotionally and can change our mood, then why couldn't it help us be better leaders? I'm here to tell you: It can. Sharing your musical mindset is like sharing a piece of who you are internally, and as leaders, it is up to us to inspire the people we serve.

How does a musical mindset help us as leaders?

1. In times of crisis: Music can offer clarity and focus.

2. In times of preparation: Using the right music can help you focus on the task.

3. In times of growth: Creating your playlists can help you avoid becoming emotionally numb and instead create a space for trust.

4. In times of celebration: You can let the music resonate within your accomplishments.

[6] https://www.gsb.stanford.edu/insights/can-your-personality-explain -your-itunes-playlist

COMPARING THE ROLE OF MUSICAL INSTRUMENTS TO BUSINESS TEAM LEADERS

As avid concertgoers, my husband and I flew to Atlanta to see one of my favorite bands, The Struts. They were playing at a quaint venue, and we arrived early for a VIP event so we could meet the band members as they were getting ready to go onstage. They all were incredibly kind as well as gifted with buckets of talent.

Since the first floor, called the pit, was standing room only, we ran upstairs and got seats in the first row of the balcony, center stage. As I was enjoying the evening, I began to take notice of the relationship between the fans and the band. The room was packed with singing fans, jumping up and down and waving their hands. When the show ended, they seemed to have left with a feeling of wanting more. As we were driving back to the hotel, with my ears still ringing, I started to think about how the musical instruments correspond to the roles of team members in the corporate world. Yes, music and business.

I began to picture in my head what it would look like if leaders *rocked* the same attention from their teams. Would results continue to grow, or would corporate brands get noticed and be remembered, like so many musicians today? I couldn't sleep with these thoughts running through my head, and that is precisely when the idea of music and leadership started to take form. I thought about each instrument and what it added to complete the band—what sound, what role it played. Does this analogy work when thinking of team members in the business world? What role does each play in business, and what sound does each bring to the table?

I started by looking up the primary role for each instrument. Then I used my love of music, basic familiarity with the instruments, and knowledge of really great musicians to help create the analogy within the realm of leadership. We will dive deeper into each business team player later, but here are the descriptions I developed that evening for each instrument in a leadership role and why.

Drums: Their primary role is to keep time, which is the pulse of the song, and to lay the song's foundation. What skills do those roles remind you of? In business, drummers are the forward thinkers of a company. They are the leaders, keeping the pulse of the company to strategically grow the business. To do this well, they usually possess a visionary trait. Drummers take the time to stop and look at the future of the business. They think beyond what currently is by creating strategies, brainstorming ideas around a plan, testing the plan, and deciding whether to risk it or not. Therefore, I am naming their Side B Legacy Behavior as **curious**. To me, this behavior complements the forward thinker or the visionary because they are always asking everyone questions, keeping tempo, laying a foundation for the future, and looking at the future goals of the company.

Lead Guitar: Its primary roles are to play the melody line, fill space, and play solos and riffs. The lead guitar is the one that takes initiative in the band, sounding authoritative and enthusiastic at the same time.

The traits that come to my mind here are accountability and dependability. Fans count on the lead guitarist to play their solo with passion. In business accountability, these traits are tough to acquire and even more difficult to teach, but passionate leaders are able to drive this behavior with ease. Therefore, a leader must be dependable and reliable, one who is clear about what they expect from themselves and others. They must measure and enforce those things which are being completed and done. This description leads us to the Side B Legacy Behavior that must show up here, which is **passionate**: a passion for people, the company, and yourself. I see every day that people who are passionate have an unending drive to get results.

Bass Guitar: Rich in deep sound, its primary roles are to accompany the drums, keep a steady rhythm, and play those honest beats that reach right into the soul. The bass guitar influences the tempo and is the forthright communicator for the music and sound.

When I thought of the bass guitar as it might relate to business, I immediately went to the rich, noticeably clear sound that the bass plays. Hearing it makes your heart feel like it is about to jump out of your chest. The bass seems to stand out while beautifully supporting the drums. When I hear the communication between the bass and the drums, its sound is so clear and true. Business leaders who communicate clearly with truth and integrity will be heard, like the loud pounding of a heartbeat, by their teams, employees, and companies. Bass guitarists are usually the band members whom people believe. When they speak, they speak with clear conviction. The Side B Legacy Behavior that must show up is staying **ethical** and having strong morals. Because once ethics are broken, so is the heart.

Piano: Its primary role is either to stand on its own, creating a beautiful sound, or accompany other instruments and provide support. When I listen to the piano, I know the notes are highly organized and the melodies put together can guide you through any conflict.

Some of the greatest pianists, Sergey Rachmaninov, Artur Rubenstein, and Martha Argerich, show us how a sense of timing and structure provides a lovely yet strong sincerity to the music. Today, when I hear "Piano Man" by Billy Joel, I can feel his sincerity and conflict in the keys played. Pianists play with such conviction and knowledge that it seems to flow right off their fingertips. To me, the leader who represents this instrument must have strong, sincere convictions and skills in conflict resolution and decision-making. A leader must be willing to make the difficult decisions that land at their office door. Typically, these are the decisions that no one else wants to make and usually involve some type of resolution. To master this Side B Legacy Behavior, you must show up as **sincere**, free from hypocrisy, and willing to accept responsibility.

Rhythm Guitar: Its primary roles are to keep the rhythmic pulse and provide part of the musical harmony. The rhythm guitar is about the paradox of planning and desiring challenge, yet collaborating well with the other instruments.

When we hear music, we trust that the sound we are hearing is what was meant. When thinking about the band, I needed to add the rhythm guitar because it is so true in providing harmony to a song. We need harmony in business, we need leaders who say what they mean and do what they say, and we need leaders we can trust. It is the leader who ensures collaboration and effectively sets goals that people (sales & operations) can achieve. If you are a leader that people trust, they understand you have their back. Then, they will go out of their way to perform better. It is with this leader that the company keeps its harmony, and the desired results ultimately become reality. The needed skills here are earning trust and bringing encouragement and motivation. The Side B Legacy Behavior that must show up is **trustworthy**. Others must be able to rely on the leader to be honest and truthful.

Vocalist: Their primary roles are to provide the song with direction and clarity and create a sound pleasing to the fans. The vocalist is frank and assertive, and their tone can be manipulated in many different ways depending on what the vocalist wants to express.

As I was thinking about the vocalists, the frontmen/women, many exceptional people came to mind. Just a few of these robust vocalists are Stevie Nicks, Freddie Mercury, David Lee Roth, Janis Joplin, and Luke Spiller. When defining this role, I pictured them with their robust, empowering energy that speaks to the audience when they are on stage. They give us hope that tomorrow will be bright. Yet, they are very calculated in their moves, outfits, and style.

In leadership, I see these leaders as ones who speak with confidence and believe the future is bright. This person's leadership is empowering, encouraging, and very focused on business strategies. The Side B Legacy Behavior is **optimistic**. This means they see the glass as always full, making it easy for others to follow them. This leader is business savvy yet cares about people.

Violin: Its primary role in any music ensemble is the melody of the music. Violins are able to transfer inspiration and emotion to the listener with a whisk of the bow. The violin, so certain about its sound, has the ability to influence and experiment with other instruments.

I thought for several days about what instrument is melodic, confident, transformative, and willing to take risks. My answer was the violin. With a chin piece and bow, the violinist can take risks in forming different sounds yet be willing to take that sound to different levels. That was it! This leader must be transformational, take risks, and be confident to experiment with new ideas. The business leader who is willing to push an envelope or two is willing to take that chance in the face of results and growth. The Side B Legacy Behavior that shows up is being **certain** and having complete conviction in experimenting and taking risks. It is in their certainty that we see their confidence to take a risk.

Saxophone: Its primary roles are to firm up tone, add a richness in voice, and charm the listener. The saxophone is made of brass; a single-reed instrument that produces sound as the mouthpiece vibrates in a warm, reflective nature.

Some of the great saxophonists include the likes of Charlie Parker, John Coltrane, Clarence Clemons, and Nubya Garcia. You can hear their voices through their instrument and tell a story with a rich sound. When I listen to the saxophone, I almost hear them listening to their own tone, like a keen self-awareness to keep playing.

I see this leader as one who actively listens and is rich in thought and reflection. As this leader listens to the tone of the people and reflects on conversation, they can instantly become gracious and thankful for who each person is individually. This leader understands each person's uniqueness, like each key on the saxophone that creates its own sound. **Gracious** is their Side B Legacy Behavior.

Harmonica: Its primary role is melody. As a versatile and compact instrument, it is easy to break out and carry. The harmonica is a free-reed wind instrument that, when played, crosses many musical genres and collaborates to support a vocal or other instruments. It is also a great instrument to begin learning tones and sounds.

I chose the harmonica because it serves as a connector, bringing people together through a melody. Although it is one everyone can *somewhat* play, only a few have become known for their talent like Stevie Wonder, Alan Wilson, Bob Dylan, or Big Mama Thornton. When you watch footage of them, you can see how they play intuitively and become one with the harmonica.

This is much like a leader who functions as an open-minded mentor/coach, is considerate of others, and provides support in every instance. This leader knows that it is the *people* who will achieve results. Leading with accountability and kindness allows that leap of faith in the service of others. The Side B Legacy Behavior that shows up is **kind,** which is a quality that is easy to carry, can be broken out at any time, and brings people together. This behavior goes a long way to serve, empower, and inspire people. This person is strong in using both intuition and knowledge to serve people.

Conga Drums: Their primary role is to supply the rhythms essential for dancing. The conga drums are usually played with the hands, and it is because of this that the sound is flexible and consistently changing. Being comfortable with the conga drums is a skill that requires risk-taking and experimenting.

I had to really take my time and understand this instrument. According to the *New World Encyclopedia*, the conga drum is a Cuban drum of African origin. I chose this instrument after recently seeing Mick Fleetwood on the final Fleetwood Mac Tour in 2019. When I saw him play, I wanted to get up and dance, even though there was no room for it. I saw the strength, adaptability, and flexibility it took for him to play the congas, using each part of his hand and the drums to produce sound.

As a leader, being flexible and adaptable is so important. Leaders are faced with obstacles and challenges each day, and having the courage to "bang on the drum" using different areas of both the drum and your hands is a valuable trait. This leader is not deterred by crises and faces objections head-on... and is usually one step ahead of any problems. Like the conga drums, this leader is not afraid but is already prepared and quickly plans to course-correct. The Side B Legacy Behavior that shows up is **courageous**. The courage to supply rhythms to dance to is the same as a leader willing to play with the sound, working within change and crisis management to accomplish the results needed.

HOW CAN MUSICAL MEMORY, MOTIVATION, AND MINDSET HELP YOU AS A LEADER?

Putting music and leadership together goes back a long time for me, and knowing the critical role music can play in your leadership is contagious. If you take your cue from music, you can create a space that is unique and likely different from what you have been shown or taught already. Learned skills, decision-making talent, and many other necessary and practical Side A competencies are needed to complete a résumé, fit a job description, and grow a business. However, those don't make up the whole picture. It is now up to you to learn your Side B Legacy Behavior as well.

Song: "All I Need"
It's the music deep in me
Nothing here to touch or see
Yet it can deeply change the view of the world
It helped complete me, show'd me where I belong
So I'm here just holding my dreams. It's all I need

Lyrics by Paula White

CHAPTER 3

SIDE A LEADERSHIP: THE HIT SONG PEOPLE HEAR

"One good thing about music,
when it hits you, you feel no pain."
—*Bob Marley*

After conducting a battery of tests, the doctor reasons that Henry's headaches seem to stem from the stress of the never-ending tasks that need to be completed. As a CEO of a large company, Henry needs to deliver a quarterly report to shareholders who want a return on their investment and healthy dividends for the quarter. In addition, the company has a lot of different projects in progress, and he needs to be on top of all of them.

As Henry is driving back from the doctor's office, he realizes he is already late for his daughter's t-ball game and calls his wife to apologize. Again. His wife, Sue, is very understanding and knows the pressure he is under at the moment. However, she also knows she can speak to Henry frankly and reminds him of the importance of family time.

"Our kids are only young once, and we haven't had a week's vacation since you started this position just over three years ago. Sure, we have had some long weekends together, but they are rarely ever disruption-free, as ongoing demands seem to escalate with your title and responsibilities. Where's the balance, Henry?"

Wouldn't you know it, just as they hang up the phone, Henry turns on the oldies station, remembering how the song he overheard in the doctor's office took him back in time. Without even realizing it, he is becoming more attuned to listening. While already beating himself up for missing out on his daughter's game, he hears "Cat's in the Cradle" by Cat Stevens begin to play. Henry, who is not normally an emotional person, starts to feel a lump in the back of his throat, and visions of unrealized vacations and lost time cause him to begin to question how he's lived up to the role of a "family man."

Henry can run a multibillion-dollar company but is falling short on his do/say ratio with his own family. This realization starts to dig at him as he pulls into the office parking lot. He dials his wife's cell phone again, but this time she doesn't answer. She is busy cheering their daughter on at her game. He leaves a message and immediately promises to find the time to take a family vacation this year and step away to the beach for some fun and sun. However, when he takes a moment to look at his calendar, he can't find a full week to vacation with his family. His calendar is booked with meetings, due dates, reports for the board, and a pending acquisition and all that entails. Henry begins to question himself, asking why there never seems to be enough time.

Henry leaves the office immediately and runs to the car. He throws his jacket in the back seat, loosens his tie, and heads north to catch the tail end of the game. As he is pulling in, he passes his wife, Sue, and daughter, who are just pulling out to go home for dinner. He decides to park, gets out of the car, heads onto the empty field, and stands there for 10 minutes (which seems more like 10 hours). Henry stares out in the distance, listening to the silence of a once very noisy field. Then, the kids and parents of the team playing in the next game begin to arrive on the field next to where he is standing.

The parents are chatting, and the kids are warming up to music. Henry can't even recognize the songs through all the laughter of the children. On his way back to the car, he knows he made the right decision to show up, even if he was too late. As he starts the car, he doesn't completely realize it, but music is entering into his being as the gift it is meant to be. He hears the song "Listen to the Music" by the Doobie Brothers and remembers that Ken, his assistant, is getting married to his partner this weekend. He decides to stop and pick up a card and gift card for their favorite restaurant but realizes he doesn't really know Ken all that well. After 10 years working with him, Henry is ashamed that he has not taken the time to get to know Ken and his fiancé on somewhat of a personal level. So, he goes to a very expensive restaurant in town and picks up a last-minute gift card.

We begin to see Henry starting to understand that when leaders focus solely on numbers and data, the opportunities to get to know their loyal and committed employees are slim and take a back seat to the grand scale of building a business. It is all about mergers and gobbling up acquisitions, squeezing out profit and avoiding loss, and looking at supply and demand and the like. Time is moving faster and faster, and if he does not slow down, he will miss a rather large part of life.

He cannot wait for the fog to lift.

Wait, I have to lift it, he thinks.

♪♪♪

I know a lot of leaders get stuck in the same place as Henry. They have all the résumé qualities and know the importance of continuing to build upon those skills and be a student of the business. This is, of course, the foundation of how great companies are built. The following are the necessary Side A skills that, as leaders, we must be particularly gifted in possessing. And that is where we begin our journey together. Think about Side A of a record—the money song, the Billboard Top 40 hit, the backbone of the release, and the one that everyone wants to see, hear, and play. Side A is the song that will make you a rock star.

Or so it seems…

Think of Side A as the hard skills or the résumé-building skills required for career growth. I have broken these skills down into three categories for our Side A discussion: results & achievement; leadership skills, behavioral competencies & traits, and leadership engagement. Let's take a look at each of these more in-depth.

RESULTS & ACHIEVEMENT

A leader's ability to achieve results stems from their internal motivation to achieve their goals. If I may be honest, the traits that are necessary to advance—grit, tenacity and drive—are nothing that can be taught; they are simply a part of who a leader is and a predictor of how much they are willing to give of themselves to achieve their goals. You could view this skill set as a leader's internal song!

LEADERSHIP SKILLS, BEHAVIORAL COMPETENCIES & TRAITS

As leaders, we are always looking to upgrade our skills and competencies to enhance our Side A résumé. These skills and competencies show our ability to focus on results and achievements in business. They are the hard skills necessary to drive revenue and grow profit, or at least this is what we are taught to believe. These are the types of qualifications most likely talked about in interviews, measured for success, and sculpted with further training. As we all know, job seekers are expected to have specific skills and traits, typically listed in a job description, to be considered for a position within a company. A list of skills and competencies a company may be looking for are:

- Good communication skills
- Problem-solving skills
- Leadership skills
- Strategic thinking
- Time-management skills
- Decision-making skills
- Prioritization and delegation skills
- Results-driven attitude
- Goal setting/achievement
- Strong business acumen
- Risk analysis
- Change and crisis management
- Mentoring/coaching and self-awareness

These skills are highly coveted and necessary competencies to demonstrate enough effective leadership and business acumen to become a Sr. Leader or CEO. These skills serve as your Side A and will afford you the opportunity to get the job done, achieve outstanding results, and grow a company. Yes, it is important to keep these skills sharp.

In addition to practical skills, employers also look for behavioral traits, such as:

- Visionary

- Accountable

- Lives with integrity

- Motivational

- Empowering of others

- Innovative

- Adaptable/flexible

- Humble

- Open-minded

- Self-disciplined

Again, these are all essential traits needed to drive a corporation forward and achieve desired results. Most leaders have these listed on their résumés as core competencies that they know will help get them through the door. Since these are "essential leadership skills," we choose to highlight our individual skillset to best exemplify our talents. We might consider these skills as our branding buzzwords, our lyrics, that show off our best song. This list encompasses both who we are and what we are capable of doing and bringing to the table.

In short, these are the popular skills and traits—the Side A track—that companies rely on to choose the best candidate and grow. You may have one, some, or all of them listed and become a highly desirable leader. Therefore, we spend most of our time upskilling these Side A traits, knowing that having these skills and competencies will increase our paycheck and make us look more desirable. We invest in our Side A traits without hesitation through taking extra courses, gaining more education, attending webinars and classes, reading books, and seeking out mentors/coaches that can help us build upon these skills and traits—for the rest of our careers.

As you build your résumé and begin to climb the corporate ladder, you are also taking the next steps to become an extraordinary leader and develop your Authentic Leadership Legacy. But there are several things that must be highlighted to ensure you are bringing your whole self to the role and not leaving the best of you behind. These highlights are the unique leadership traits that you bring to the role so your team can perform better.

For example, let's consider the role of a VP of Sales. What Side A traits, skills, and competencies might a company look for as they interview candidates, and what is the candidate looking for in a company to ensure a good fit for both? Here is a brief review of the Side A skills and competencies a corporation may seek from a VP of Sales:

For a VP of Sales, a company may look for a person that is results-driven, analytical, adaptable, detail-oriented, initiative-taking, and able to multitask. In regards to the VP's people and communication skill set, they may look for effective collaboration, listening skills, writing skills, great communication, and negotiating skills.

Your leadership traits play a large role in how well you fit within a company and vice versa. These are traits that are uniquely related to you as a person, traits that are not easy to train; instead, they come naturally. These might include naturally encouraging diversity, empowering others, a strong moral compass, strategic thinking, or being a team builder.

So, we can see that skills and competencies are important, and we focus on them more often. We know that we have other traits that we bring to the table that are innately us. But that is where we often stop because we know that 2+2 =4, and the equation is complete—or is it? I want to share with you there is more, so much more to that equation. Just like music, we need to stretch beyond what we know, like, and listen to in order to understand how to bring our whole self to our career. So, let's move the discussion forward and talk about five essential qualities to master before we turn over the record to Side B.

LEADERSHIP ENGAGEMENT

There are companies that are extraordinary, great, or just good—and then some not so good. So, what separates the good from the extraordinary?

I can share with you from experience that good companies have worn out their Side A record because they continue to play the same song each year, and it now has skips and scratches. They continue to engage in promoting the same style of leadership and business, never asking if the way they are doing things is the best. It's the thought process of, "We are doing it this way because it's the way we have always done it." These companies have played the same song loudly each year, and the whole company is singing every lyric in unison, and the results are… you guessed it: good. But we want to be better than good! Tried and true may be a good plan; however, the extraordinary companies are willing to tap into the beginnings of Side B.

Side B leadership can truly make a company extraordinary and open doors into possibilities a purely Side A style cannot. Now, Side A skills are necessary, but where the opportunity lies and where the switch to Side B happens is when a company engages the "people skills" of Side A, therefore attuning themselves to this type of thinking and skill set. Extraordinary companies empower leaders, practice active listening, understand that failure is learning, mentor protégés, and network. These companies find themselves on the verge of changing their leadership record to Side B.

Are You Really Listening?

Active listening is a Side A skill that is often underutilized; however, to fully engage your Side B Behavior, it must be mastered. Without active listening skills, your Side B won't matter as much because you won't be serving your people first. Active listening helps you truly understand what people are saying in conversations and meetings (and not just what you *want* to hear, or *think* you hear). Not truly listening will lead to plenty of misinformation or information you need that you missed hearing.

Since active listening is an important skill to master to reach Side B, I wanted to find out more about the topic of listening for leaders, so I spoke with Amy Balog, CEO and Executive Coach of ConnextionPoint. Yes, if you're thinking *that Amy*, you'd be right. My coach. She has been instrumental in helping others transform their listening skills with intentionality and has been featured on many podcasts, speaking about this very topic.

Amy's very first comment to me in our meeting will set the stage and help you understand the importance of active listening. She said, "Listening is a state of being, not a skill. We have more powerful choices for understanding, and when we realize the impact of listening, we can step into who we are as a listener." Think about that for a moment. When we know how to listen, we have more choices for action, reaction, reflection, or simply hearing people.

In the ever-moving and chaotic world we live in, who are we as listeners? Our brain is always moving and working too. Given that, how can we control some of our own thoughts to focus on listening and not just wait for an opening to say what we are wanting to say? But even then, we are often thinking about what we want to say so we don't forget.

Well, Amy has a great suggestion for this challenge too. I tried it and now use it consistently. Back when 9/11 occurred, the news media created a news scroll at the bottom of the TV screen to keep us informed even while listening to other important news topics. Amy suggests, "To listen, a beautiful technique to use when talking to someone is to imagine a

TV screen. The person you are talking with would be on the big screen, and your thoughts drop into the banner [at the bottom]. Scroll down below and let them go ahead."

As we continued our conversation, Amy spoke about the art of *unexpected* listening. This is a beneficial teaching for leaders with their own agendas who are pulled into meetings. Amy says, "We expect to go into a boardroom, event, meeting, or conversation ready to perform. [We think] *I have things to say, a position to give, and opinions to protect, so my mind and thoughts are ready.* However, when we go in open and ready to listen, better conversations unfold, and ideas are birthed that can take us in a direction that we didn't know was available." Yes, unexpected listening is a more advanced level of listening and creates room for the generation of new ideas and productive brainstorming to happen.

As a leader, when you master the ability to recognize when you really need to dialogue with someone or when you only need to receive information, you are beginning to understand how to show up in a conversation. It is important to go into the conversation knowing what kind of listener you're going to be at the beginning.

I was learning so much that I asked Amy one more question: What are the consequences that we could face in the future if we do not sharpen our listening skills?

She answered, "Well, we are living in a world that is hungry to be heard, and we have a lot of voices speaking at once, but we are losing our resonance because we're not listening. The consequences are profound disconnection."

Powerful!

Amy's top tips for listening:

1. Have intentionality.

2. Consider listening as a state of being, not a skill.

3. Be fully present.

4. Use the scroll bar.

Failure as a Risk

Another essential Side A skill to master is that of understanding the difference between failure and risk. Why? Leaders tend to be either risk-favorable or risk-averse. However, to be successful and transfer these skills to Side B, it is necessary to have a balanced mindset for opportunities. I am fortunate to have had a conversation with Mark Dougherty, CFO, COO, and Business Development (M&A), about his success and how he approaches new ideas and execution. When is the right time? What is the right mindset to achieve success?

When I first sat down with Mark, my initial question was, "How do you know when a risk is worth taking?"

His answer was quite simple. "Many leaders choose to forgo a process. Most risks are worth taking. The key is to put the plan in writing with enough detail to get to a formal recommendation. The process of writing the document will clearly point out if it is a good idea or if it is too risky. If you are not sure, you have not done enough of the detailed thinking yet. Invest in writing the recommendation, and it will become noticeably clear."

Sometimes we jump, react, or make decisions based on our gut or intuition; however, if it is something new or may be a risk for the company, due diligence is important. A good decision is based on doing your homework first!

We went on to discuss failure as an opportunity and the mindset that is necessary to execute a risk. Mark believes one must make a clear distinction between poor execution and an opportunity that was less than expected. It is easy to recover from a failure if the execution was there. However, what is difficult is when the execution is poor. When there is clarity, and the execution is 100% present, then failure is simply not an option. This is a clear distinction that a leader should take to heart; it goes along with the old saying by Benjamin Franklin, "If you fail to plan, you plan to fail."

Understandably, we all want to do the right thing and play it safe, but where does safe get us? There is a Paul Simon song titled "Slip Slidin' Away" which talks about how we are sometimes so close, yet so far from our success. I used to think that failure was the end of it all, which made me fearful of speaking up. However, it is within those failures that we learn valuable lessons, and taking risks is important to your success. Both risk taking and failure will teach us valuable lessons and help get us to an endpoint.

Thinking along this vein, I asked Mark, "What is your definition of failure and risk when it comes to business opportunities?"

"Risk is merely trying something with an unknown outcome, and that is a part of business we should do every day!

If you want to accomplish something worthwhile, take the risk. Failure, in the business sense, can be falling short of expectations, but that is OK! Learn from it and move on." Meaning if you planned and executed the plan, but the risk didn't work—move on. Leaders who are willing to try new ideas or take a risk are the ones that eventually find the answer or solution to a problem that is a huge win for themselves and their company.

Since I was already speaking with Mark, I wanted to ask this final question.

"What would you tell a new leader about failure and risk?"

He answered, "The most important lesson for leaders is to hire great people. Don't hire what you need today, don't hire what you can afford, and don't hire somebody like you. You must clearly understand the job requirements and the skill sets necessary to be successful and hire to that. And if you have the right team and you have the right boss, you don't have risk—all you have is opportunity."

Mark's top tips for taking risks:

1. Make a formal plan.
2. Execute the plan.
3. Hire right.

The Upside of Mentoring

The Side A skill of mentoring is a first step toward serving people, and mastering this skill by putting people first will jump-start your Side B Trait. Who better to speak to about this subject but one of my first manager mentors, Larry Reeves, COO of American Association of Inside Sales Professionals? He certainly helped me kick off my journey of learning to lead. Much to my surprise, I found out that his passions include music! He is a bassist and has played with and/or led numerous bands, and has had the good fortune to have studied with several of the world's finest musicians.

I believe all his diverse experiences have positioned him to develop a unique perspective. He and I both agree that mentoring has taken a back seat over the past decade. I asked him, "For those looking for a mentor, where should they start?"

Larry advised, if possible, to try not to limit yourself to just one mentor. He says, "Having a mentor within your organization, which is definitely something I would recommend, can be a great thing and provide valuable insight directly related to your current role/organization/situation. However, it has some downsides as well. For example, you have to remember you still have an employer/employee relationship, and you would need to be careful talking about sensitive work-related issues. You would also need to guard against freely showing any thoughts or feelings that could somehow negatively impact your position within the company."

"Having said that," he added, "I do believe having a strong relationship with an executive-level person within your organization can be very valuable to both development and advancement. I would suggest speaking with your immediate manager, an HR representative, or if you have an individual you would like to learn from, approach them and ask them directly. The key here is to simply ask. Try it, and you might just be surprised by the results."

This led us to talking about looking for a mentor outside of your organization and the value that brings. Larry said, "A person outside your organization can sometimes bring a fresh, broader, more neutral perspective and will typically also allow you to speak freely and openly about your issues and situation. In many instances, this is what is needed. However, a possible downside is that they don't know your business or industry very well. Trade associations, social networking, or local groups are some potential resources. In addition, today there are professionals available for hire that can help as well."

Larry and I went on to discuss how mentors should be matched, and I asked, "How do you know what types of qualities someone should look for in a mentor?"

His advice is, first, knowing what you want to (or need to) get out of the relationship is essential. From there, you want to seek someone who has those "qualifications." He suggests that you look for someone who is successful at doing what you want to do. Also, from a personality perspective, he feels it is important to find someone who wants to give back and matches your "style," but be careful there, too. It's typically good to "like" your mentor, but there may be instances where the relationship might not be that important. If the mentor can provide valuable guidance/advice, at the end of the day, that is truly paramount in a mentor/protégé relationship. Some examples of this may be when someone hires a mentor or perhaps a company/organization has a formal mentoring program.

Again, the key is to find someone that can help you get what you need. Remember, you do not have to limit yourself to one mentor, especially as you move throughout your career.

As we continued, I asked, "On the other hand, what qualities does a mentor consider or look for in a protégé?" Larry speaks of this from a personal perspective and says that his most successful relationships have been with individuals that have a good work ethic, are serious about their personal development, and have a good idea of what they are seeking.

Many protégés are looking for help in confidence or encouragement, so it is important that a mentor listen, facilitate, guide, and encourage that thought process. Larry encourages this process by listening—understanding what the protégé is saying and their situation is key. He typically starts by asking a lot of questions to bring forward any issues, as well as discussing potential options and outcomes, which, in turn, often reveals the most likely scenario or path for their desired outcome.

Larry's top tips to start a journey of professional growth are:

1. Have a positive attitude, for the way you react makes the difference.

2. Take care of your people; your role is to help them succeed.

3. Communicate with clarity.

4. Know your business; plan for the best case, worst case, and most likely outcome of your decisions and actions.

Is Networking an Important Side A Skill?

The last essential Side A skill is the importance of networking. Mastering this skill will help your Side B Trait tenfold as a true people-first skill. As a leader, networking will serve your teams by experiencing other people and gaining the knowledge of whom to talk to when the people you serve have a particular need to address or expanding resources for your team's education. Naturally, I turned to an expert of networking, Ed Porter, Chief Revenue Officer, Board Member, Mentor, and Chapter President, to name a few. There really isn't anything Ed cannot do because he knows who to go to or will find someone to help you do what is needed. Ed is a "master networker," and when I had the opportunity to sit and have pizza with Ed, I was curious as to what goes on in his head.

I wanted to understand when leaders begin to master this skill, what it looks like, and how you know you are ready to move to Side B. I began by asking him this: "When thinking about the term 'networking,' what do you envision in your head?"

"I have always been a student first. I am a curious person, and I want to know and learn. That is why I go to events—to network. However, networking is not about me. It is more in the vein of going up to a table of people who are talking and beginning to ask questions. Sometimes it's as simple as, 'Hey, what do you do? How did you wind up there? What do you like about *(insert topic)*, or what do you not like about it?' It is about understanding how people wind up in the places they live, how they found their jobs, and, of course, what other adventures make them who they are as a person." I absolutely believe that the more we understand people, the more we can relate to them, and the better we tap into our Side B Trait.

Ed and I discussed that the most important thing about networking is to be genuinely interested in people. In fact, that is how you find similarities. For example, Ed and I were attending the same conference over eight years ago, and in the very last session, I stood up and asked the facilitator a question. Ed had the same question and, after the session, tracked me down and introduced himself. The funny thing was, we both are from Columbus, Ohio, the home of the Ohio State Buckeyes.

We continued to talk and later started a local AA-ISP Chapter together. Ed explained that he always starts his conversations with uncovering how people wind up in Ohio. He shared his philosophy about hearing a person's backstory. People come from all over, and it is always interesting to find out why they landed in Ohio. Listening to their interesting backstories might give you insight into who they are as a person.

For example, maybe someone transferred in for a career promotion, or maybe they are here because of a sick family member. Either way, you are learning and communicating with people. Ed observed, "When we communicate with others, we become more enlightened to serve others." He makes a great point that not many people network from a people-first perspective. Instead, they look to make it about how the other person can help them. Using a people-first approach while building your networking skills is critical to understanding and advancing your Side B Trait.

Next, I asked Ed about networking for business purposes. He said, "There is no shame in saying 'I want business.' That's fine, but just know that business happens organically. It has to do with the fact that, ultimately, you are solving a problem. Do not force it. Do not push it. Do not try to be Mr./Miss/Mrs. Handshake—that just does not serve you well. Listen, networking must be authentic. Do not do it just because you feel it is what you must do. However, if you want to but feel you are not any good at it, then learn." He makes another excellent point in that, to master this skill, we need to be authentic and listen. This sounds a lot like what we've been talking about to be an extraordinary leader—yes?

Ed went on to talk about the fact that the most successful people are networkers because of another reason—not just to put themselves out there. Do not do it for the notoriety because those who are successful measure success not by the number of likes on social media but by a life influenced or a connection realized.

He finished our conversation by sharing some wisdom: "Ultimately, network for yourself." I took this to mean, network to experience others and intentionally learn about people, not for what they can do for you, but for the sheer experience.

Ed's top tips for authentic networking:

1. Be genuinely curious and interested in people.
2. Be interested in and focus on the relationship.
3. There is no shame in networking to further your business, but let the conversation happen organically.

THERE IS MORE TO LEADERSHIP

Two weeks before the COVID-19 lockdown, I was in the airport waiting for my plane to arrive at the gate. I made sure to only bring a carry-on and my laptop. I did this so that when I landed, I could get straight to the hotel, set up, and get prepared for my interview with Duane Cummings—the man who helped define my perspective on leadership. As you may recall from earlier, I was attending an executive retreat when he said those four simple words that turned a light bulb on and forever impacted my leadership style: "Flip the organizational chart."

As I was waiting, I got in my head and became extremely nervous. I mean, can you blame me? I was going to speak with the gentleman who turned my leadership mindset upside down! My stomach started to settle with the venti decaf caramel cloud macchiato in my hands and a plane ready to board, and I began thinking about the questions I prepared. Were they good enough? *Sit tight, Paula, they are fine*, I told myself. Prepare for the worst, right? But the nervous questions kept coming. *What if I find that Duane was only giving a speech and didn't mean what he said? What if FtOC was only a concept he talked about? No, I have to trust that he honestly believes in leading by putting others first, or the whole impact of FtOC would be a fraud—a mistake, just like so many I have seen before.*

Before I knew it, we landed in Oklahoma City, OK. I made it to the hotel about 9 p.m. and was going to settle in for a night's rest before the big day. However, as I walked into the room, to my surprise, there was a card from Duane and his wife, Kim, welcoming me to Oklahoma.

Drop the mic. This man is for real. (Which I already knew!)

The next day, I got dressed and ready to spend the day with both Duane and Kim. We toured around Oklahoma City, visited the Memorial, then it was off to lunch, where the interview would take place. I pulled out my phone with the questions on it and started to record. We were there for over an hour and a half, just talking about business, leaders, and life. It was more than I imagined. He was exactly as I believed him to be, and his wife was lovely.

What I have known for a very long time, but honestly was afraid to say out loud for fear of again sounding weak or immature, was that there is more to leadership than skills and competencies. In fact, you can achieve desired results by being gracious, you can lead by example with optimism, and your team can have 100% trust in you. This is the next level of leadership—extraordinary leadership. You truly can have it all: love, leadership, and results. You only need to flip the organizational chart, flip your record, and understand your greatest strength is on Side B.

This is where I will ask you to listen to "Have It All" by Jason Mraz. Remember, leadership influence and company culture start with the leader: you!

Song: Side B
Maybe, I should have not let you see my warmth and empathy
Did that make me look weak or does that make me so unique
It is my belief in time that we should be the ones who lead
And that, my friend, is on Side B

Lyrics by Paula White

CHAPTER 4

SIDE B LEADERSHIP: TIME TO REMIX YOUR LEADERSHIP STYLE

"How is it that music can, without words,
evoke our laughter, our fears,
our highest aspirations?"
—*Jane Swan*

A few weeks have passed since Henry made the promise to find a week for his family vacation. Sue, his wife, has been looking at a few travel brochures and asking each evening what he would like to do, but the pressure of the upcoming board meeting has been his focus and priority both day and night. However, what has gone unnoticed is Sue's frustration of yet another family promise that has been put on the back burner.

Since she has already talked to the kids about going on vacation, Sue intends to keep her promise and books a trip to St. John, Virgin Islands, without Henry. While this has caused many sleepless nights for both of them, Henry agrees that they should go without him—the kids aren't getting any younger, and he wants them to have the experience and spend time together.

Now, Henry is definitely feeling torn between two worlds, one of business and one with his family, which is something he has not felt before. It's overwhelming.

♪♪♪

It is the day of the board meeting. All the board members flew into New York for two full days of progress updates and strategic planning. Overall, the meeting goes well, and the board members are pleased with the results. They are tracking slightly ahead of plan, not necessarily from revenue, but operation cost-cutting plans, and fortunately, no human capital was affected. The company still has six months to pull off an aggressive goal, and Henry believes that with all hands in, it will happen.

On his flight home, Henry knows it is going to take everyone's 100% focus and participation at the company to finish the fiscal year strong and decides to call a meeting with the four senior executive leaders. He asks them to prepare a "State of Department" memo to share with the team, so each executive will be on the same "sheet of music" and prepared to drive the results. The presentation is to include an updated plan of action for the final six months of the fiscal year, a pipeline analysis, course correction plans, if needed, and employee stack rankings (shown by the graphic below).

Three hours into this meeting, the operations department head, Clint, begins with the manager stack rank. Henry is very surprised to see Pat ranked as a "D" employee. Being curious,

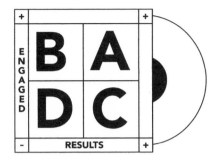

he asks, "Why has Pat gone from being an 'A' player for six years to a 'D' in a matter of months? His results look good, and he seems engaged."

The answer was simple. Clint replies, "Pat is not engaged, and his results are good but stagnant. I am not seeing the same growth trends as in years past."

This conversation could have ended right then in that room, and Pat would probably have been fired in a few months. Since Henry is beginning to transform his leadership style, he asks Ken, his assistant, into his office and requests that he schedule two half-hour blocks of time so he can turn on his radio, declutter his thoughts, and breathe. He is trying to reduce daily stress and has been using these half-hour blocks to gain clarity by clearing his mind of daily tasks.

When the music comes on, he connects his phone to his Bluetooth speakers and flips through playlists and songs that he is connecting with at that moment. He is actively listening to the lyrics, the melody, and the bass guitar, his favorite instrument. During one of these blocks, Henry recalls that Pat started with the company around the same time as he did and knows his work ethic and attitude from working closely with him in the past. Pat's ranking did not sit well with Henry. Something doesn't sound right, doesn't feel right.

After reflecting, Henry calls Clint into his office to find out if there is something going on with Pat in his personal life. Clint doesn't offer much information apart from stating that his execution has been lacking, and he's seemed distracted for the past six months. "Maybe he is looking for a new job," Clint adds.

Henry asks Clint to schedule a meeting for the three of them in his office.

The next day, the trio sits in Henry's office, and the conversation starts with niceties and small talk. Henry asks how everything is going and wants to know if there is anything he can help with currently. Pat sits very still, pauses with deep reflection, and with a tight grip on the chair arms, he shakes his head and says, "Thank you. It has been tough lately."

What Pat does not express is that his nephew passed away suddenly, his wife is grieving while working long hours as the director of sales at a local distribution company, their kids are getting an expensive college education, his mother is living at his home, and he was recently informed of some health concerns of his own.

Needless to say, it has been difficult for Pat to bring his whole self to work.

SOMETIMES YOU NEED TO LISTEN

Listen, business leadership is a time-consuming career that requires you to use all your hard Side A skills at every moment and at every meeting or encounter. Given that, when somebody says, "Hey, let's talk about the touchy-feely side of servant leadership," we immediately dismiss that conversation as unnecessary and place it on the back burner, never to be discussed. In many corporations, opening up about your personal life and interests is not favorable. You don't want to come across as complaining, unmotivated, or self-promoting. Thus, avoiding such topics appears to be a safer approach.

Unfortunately, this is precisely the type of culture we live in, where many employees live in fear at work. Fear of losing their jobs to technology, fear of expressing an emotion that may be warranted, fear of leadership. Our workforce is highly fatigued, disconnected, and uncertain about their future.

If you're in leadership, I need you to know this: Sometimes, you just need to take your manager hat off for a few minutes and listen.

Now, hear me out. I am not suggesting that everyone should come in and lay down all their good, bad, and ugly for the world to see. It is not my philosophy that we all need to sing "Hakuna Matata"; I will leave that to *The Lion King*. However, if you, as a leader, have a good, honest, hardworking employee, it just might be worth your time to have a simple, courageous conversation, without judgment, to ask if something is going on with them.

When good leaders remix their leadership style to become invested in the people they serve, they become extraordinary. They then begin to see with greater clarity the gifts they bring to inspire and motivate others. It is with that knowledge that you, as a leader, are "Learning to Fly", as the Tom Petty song says. Give that song a listen and see how you can fly in leadership. When we take the opportunity to talk, see, and hear more, we begin to know more, which then allows us to serve more completely. It is armed with this knowledge and understanding of people that we realize music holds power in unleashing our Side B. It is in the musical memories, musical motivations, and musical mindset that we can prepare to remix our leadership style.

My advice to any leader, coach, or person, really, is to say it is your job to uncover the best aspects of the people around you. And here's the catch: They will not all look like you, act like you, or be just like you. We all have different seats at the table, so listen to the many voices around you (and don't forget to hear your own). You just might get a better understanding and a loyal employee from it! I challenge you to embrace some of those "touchy-feely" conversations as they will open your eyes. This skill is not just for HR; it is for extraordinary leaders like you. It is the next level of your Authentic Leadership Legacy and language. If you balk at this initially, try to start slowly. There are consequences to only leading from Side A. Trust me!

THE BONUS TRACK

We all have different leadership styles. What works for one person may not work for the next. Leaders are not born, factory-made, or educated the same. I mean, how boring would that be?! Leaders come into their own at their own time and not always with the company's coaching.

When I first became a manager, the coaching I received looked a little something like this:

- Emulate person X
- Be pragmatic
- Be tactical
- Be strategic
- Be hands-on
- Know your business
- Stop being so motherly
- Don't be so emotional

Great, noted. I can work on those things. But *how* do I become the leader you all want me to be? Hello! Help! Will somebody teach me?

At the end of the day, I wanted to understand the way leaders speak, how they act, how they know when and when *not* to speak up, and how they earn a seat at the table.

I thought I had to behave a certain way and talk in some type of secret leadership language and enjoy cigars. Surely that was how I'd climb to the next level, right? Again, the short answer was no.

We often try to be the leader we are "supposed" to be according to other people. However, what happens when we try to measure up to other people's standards is that we lose touch with who we truly are. We default to inauthenticity and are only focused on getting ahead, which will be more challenging each day we try to be someone we aren't meant to be. When we don't lead from our mind, heart, gut (intuition), and make decisions for the people we serve, it is easy to become a chameleon. We walk around wearing a mask, and one day, that will catch up with us. Eventually, we start to see someone very different in the mirror.

In other words, someone else is singing our song.

Early in my career, I was a "keep your head down and let results speak for you" woman. However, I wasn't getting the promotions and pay raises that others who started after me were. I began to notice that they were all outspoken—the squeaky wheel, you might say. Then I remembered a leader I looked up to say, "It is important to talk about *your* accomplishments, goals, and what you were doing in order to get the promotion."

To be very honest with you, that wasn't me. I loved my career and wanted to keep growing, but unfortunately, I was waiting around for the tap on the shoulder. That's just not how it works anymore.

So, I decided to try this self-promotion idea, talking about my ideas, goals, strategies, team accomplishments, and my Side A skills. But what I didn't realize was that, as I spoke of my ideas, goals, strategies, and team accomplishments, I wasn't doing it *"right"* or for the *"right"* reasons. Instead, I made it all about me. I began to feel very ugly, and my heart was slowly breaking. In many ways, this was truly unnatural for me and caused me a lot of turmoil because I watched and believed that if you want to go somewhere, you've got to promote yourself. Additionally, I didn't feel I could talk about it. However, as years went on, I found that most leaders don't know how to coach other leaders to properly balance hard and soft skills to inspire and encourage people while holding them accountable with a disciplined approach. *Note:* This is how you get promoted!

As I plugged along, I felt I was becoming narcissistic in some instances. My head was spinning while I was trying everyone's suggestions and their approaches, but in the end, I couldn't recognize myself anymore—let alone understand what type of leader I had become to fit in. I had lost my authenticity, and I was drowning under the weight of others' expectations. Nothing made sense anymore.

Grasping at straws, I found a variety of books on modern leadership. They touched on a multitude of topics, including networking, adversity, diversity, persuasion, negotiation, and strategic thinking. I read a ton of great books, but still had no answer to my question: How do I become the leader I want to be? Now, I know there are books that talk about the need to develop yourself from the inside out, and books to uncover your internal superpowers or discover your gifts. But I didn't choose them at first because I was afraid they would expose me as weak, motherly, and emotional. You know, the very labels I was trying desperately to avoid.

I found myself buying into the same logic many others have: that who we *are* is second best to what we *do* and accomplish.

My friend, I want to tell you that this is a bold-faced lie.

So, is being motherly, nurturing, or even going so far as being kind, with a hint of discipline and respect, bad?

No! I will take that all day long!

What I want you to realize is that even when you are faced with a potentially "negative" corporate label, it's okay. You'll need to dig deeper to find out who you are and why your behavior may be seen as weak when, in reality, you're extraordinarily strong. It is not important to impress the people around you; it is important that you know who you are at the core—and if you don't yet understand, I'll say it again: hire an executive coach! I did, and it was the best thing I could have done for myself.

What I have learned through my journey of stumbling through figuring out who I am as a leader is that I only ever wanted someone to believe in me. And that, my friend, starts on Side B. It is remixing your behaviors that makes you strong enough to tear away the mask and return to your authentic self.

Side B, the bonus track of leadership, is a personal journey that will look different for each person, just like our carefully curated playlists on Pandora, Amazon Music, Apple Music, iTunes, or Spotify. As you begin to dig in, I want you to imagine your leadership skills like you do your playlists—by taking all the songs you like from a few albums, putting them together, and ditching the rest.

PIVOTING TO SIDE B:
THE REMIX TO TRANSFORM

Interestingly enough, no one knows when it's the right or wrong time to pivot or, as I like to call it, **transform**. This pivot is one you make to become the extraordinary leader who is more engaged.

I was able to have dinner with Angela Raub, CEO of ARC Consulting, on a Sunday evening in Atlanta. She explained to me that her weekends are precious to her health and well-being, and I was honored she chose to sit down with me and give her insight on pivoting and leadership. Angela leads with a servant leadership mentality, and her favorite phrase for any team and herself is "unconditional love." She believes that is precisely where we need to start because when you give unconditional love, you are an *inclusive* leader. And through inclusion, we surround ourselves with diverse friends and people who help us develop, cause us to think differently, and help us to become better leaders and people. This is the touchy-feely stuff that is necessary to uncover in yourself. This is your remix!

She explained that we actually pivot every single day. We pivot on diets, food tastes, and clothing depending on things like the weather, seasonal produce, and trends. However, it is within the *extreme* pivots that we transform, and these are usually triggered by a specific event. The best thing to do in the event of an extreme pivot is to be still, be silent, and sit in the struggle. I will be the first to admit that sitting in the uncomfortableness of the situation doesn't always feel good.

However, in this, you are being pressed, but you will *not* be broken.

In extreme pivoting such as job or leadership changes, self-awareness can either be rewarding or destroying. We either accept and grow with our ever-changing self, or we find ourselves limited to one way of thinking. Sometimes it is valuable to change things up and get uncomfortable. When this happens, we begin to feel something; just because we don't know *what* we are feeling doesn't mean we are *not* feeling. Here is where music can help us tap into those feelings.

The first question to ask yourself when you're facing a transition is this: Why are you pivoting? Is it to run? Is it for financial reasons or to gain success? Is it a forced pivot? Or is it the best kind of pivot—one made for self-awareness and growth? This would be a pivot you're choosing to explore, one that is at the forefront of your mind for your growth. Like me asking you to remix your leadership style to include Side B, the choice to make this pivot is yours and yours alone.

Now, I believe there is no right or wrong time to pivot; there is no silver bullet or one way to do things. For me, it started with finding my inspiration, and it hit me with one song.

One night, sitting in a car, drained from work after my dad had passed away, I was crying, not knowing my next steps in my life. Then, suddenly, there was my answer—in the form of the song "(Sittin' On) the Dock of the Bay" by Otis Redding. I looked in the rearview mirror, wiped my tears away, and knew I was ready to pivot. The lyrics hit me just right, and I brushed off my negative emotions and dove into "courage," the courage to be me.

The impact of that song was unique to me in that moment, and I heard what I needed to hear. I will also say that there are often other catalysts that help people to pivot, such as a painting, a quote they read, or a podcast they hear. The key is to open your mind to see and listen for those moments of change.

It was during that season in my life that I chose to turn the music back on, and it helped me to be still, be silent, and sit in the struggle. Listening to the music helped me, much like meditation, to sit in the discomfort and allow my brain to wander and declutter all the stories I wanted to forget—the ones that I filed away in my brain for another day. I had to face them alone, and alone I did. As I began to close the chapter of grieving my dad and listening to the stories in my head, I also began to understand this was my personal pivot story that has led me to grow and come out on the other side. This led to my leadership remix!

Create a Leadership Playlist

Most people pivot to using their Side B Legacy Behavior when they are older—after they have been in leadership roles for a long time. This is the time when leaders tend to reflect on their careers and choices and begin to see how their journey played out. However, these leaders will have missed out on many benefits they could have reaped earlier in their careers by pivoting to their Side B much sooner.

For us, as leaders, showing our Side B Legacy Behavior will be incredibly impactful to the people we serve and will inspire new leaders to begin their own pivoting journey earlier. Begin a "leadership playlist" by taking all your favorite songs that motivate you and remind you of who you are naturally as a leader. It is in this process of uncovering music you enjoy that you get to individually choose songs that will represent your leadership style and creativity and open your mind to focusing on people. I see a future where people come first, and it is delightful. Your transformation will happen when you least expect it, and it will only happen when you are ready to listen to the voice inside.

Why is this important? In recent years, huge upheavals like COVID-19 called for empathy from their leaders. Not all leaders are naturally skilled in empathy, but may have another positive quality to express. For instance, some leaders are curious, optimistic, ethical, trustworthy, sincere, certain, or courageous; all of these are very important skills to show others as well. What if we took their particular quality or skill that brings out the best in them to serve others? The results of them exhibiting that quality would be powerful. If we call for authenticity in leadership, let's call for them behaving in what leads them to their best selves, and that does not look the same for every leader.

It is important to create a leadership playlist that is personally impactful and represents the best part of you. For example, your leadership playlist could include "Good Riddance (Time of Your Life)" by Green Day or "Where Are We Now" by Five Star Iris. Both songs reflect on what is, what was, and what could be. If you listen to the lyrics, you may find inspiration or an answer to your questioning if it's time to pivot in your career. Then you may add "Shiny Happy People" by R.E.M. or "Bright Side of the Road" by Van Morrison. The possibilities are endless, as your playlist is incredibly unique to your journey.

With today's technology, future leaders are fortunate to have available streaming music platforms like Spotify, iTunes, Pandora, or Amazon Music. Aspiring leaders, you can tap into creating a leadership playlist early, taking into consideration those songs that bring you joy, motivation, and inspiration. Leaning into the leader you were meant to be and creating opportunity to uncover your Side B Behavior earlier in your career will truly help and impact the people under and around you. What an amazing and full career you could enjoy by empowering others and serving those you lead to produce extraordinary results.

How Do We Start?

Contrary to popular belief, it is not a laundry list of tasks, skills, or ideas that help us remix our leadership style, create a leadership playlist, and lean into our Authentic Leadership Legacy. Rather, we can start simply by answering the question poised perfectly by The Who in their popular song "Who Are You". In the context of leadership, have you ever answered that question?

Who are you as a leader? Who do you want to be?

Do you know the answers to those questions? If you don't yet, you're not alone. Understanding who you are as a leader is difficult to define and an ever-changing part of growth. Let's start here: When you look in the mirror, what do you see? Do you see a stranger looking back at you, as I once did? Do you pick out your mask depending on the day? Do you think to yourself, *This is not the path I had originally set out on*?

I want you to visualize the following scenario for me.

You walk into the gym, put your earbuds in, and hit "play." Did you immediately have a song in mind when you pressed "play"? I'll bet you did. That's because we choose music to fit the moment. We choose what is going to motivate us in the current situation or fit the environment we're trying to create. Why do you think Spotify, Pandora, and Apple Music put so much time and care into curating very moment-specific playlists for their listeners? I can bet we all have a wide array of playlists living on our phones—one for the gym, a romantic date, a quiet night in, a rainy mood collection. Depending on the situation, you'll listen to what is calming, motivating, or sometimes even uncomfortable!

Now, think about how building a leadership playlist will empower you to adopt a Side B Legacy Behavior that shows up daily to serve those around you. Remember, everyone is unique, and your Side B Behaviors may include any combination of the following: curiosity, passion, trustworthiness, high ethics, optimism, sincerity, courage, certainty, graciousness, or kindness. Start with creating or following *one* playlist that will help you embody being present in a specific behavior like optimism, passion, courage, etc. *(HINT: I have already started a Spotify list for each behavior.)* If you prefer to begin one yourself, I included a few tips in Chapter 6 on how to start.

After you have a great leadership playlist started, then ask yourself this: What can I add to my playlist today? Or better yet, what do I have on my playlist that can be a benefit to those around me?

Not only will a personal leadership playlist help us step into a behavior quickly, but we can also create a playlist for our team goals. As a leader, I used to create a "sales theme" each year, and I would add a new playlist to my repertoire for each fiscal year. Depending on the theme and sales goals we were working towards, each playlist had its own sound, theme song, and many breakthrough songs for big moments. The playlist can be followed by the team to energize, inspire, and motivate them. It's time to start thinking about how music can develop your Side B Behavior and affect change with people, goals, and results. So, I will ask you: Are you planning to start with a personal leadership playlist or create a team theme playlist?

SIDE B REMIX: THE CUSTOMER EXPERIENCE

Extraordinary leaders are like corporate musicians—they act as a conductor of sorts when they show up in their Side B Legacy Behavior to impact people every day. Taking this a step further, how a leader serves their people from ceiling to floor (a metaphor I use because I don't believe in top to bottom) impacts customer experience.

Fans First

Concerts are not just about the band playing outstanding music or having a date night; they are an *experience*. It is more about having a mutual agreement with your fan base, which, in this case, is your customers. Of course, they want to hear great music, but they also want to feel close to the band and be treated with respect when the band performs authentically—and, in return, the band will feed off that energy.

I spoke with Cody Carson and Maxx Danziger from the band Set It Off about what it means to them to be on stage playing for their fans. Maxx Danziger, the drummer, feels he has the best seat/view in the house because he is able to see the entire band *and* the crowd. What he enjoys most is looking into the audience to see their reaction. He tries to focus on a few that look to be having the time of their lives and feeds off that energy to make it a better show for them.

Cody Carson, the lead singer, musician, and songwriter, lives for the experience onstage. For the 13 years he has been playing, one thing has never changed for him: the connection between the artist and the fans. That connection is what inspires him to give more and create an exceptional experience. He says the experience is cathartic—that for the hour or so he is performing, he gives his all, and the crowd gives it back (with their energy and participating in the songs). He says it is something you just can't describe.

Now, imagine having that type of experience with your customers! Do you think it would increase results? I certainly do—that is, if it's real and the company lays it all out there while "performing" for their customers. After all, customers buy based on what they imagine or know your product or service can do for them. The "feel" is more important than the process. Thus, if you lay it all out there, they will believe that your product will perform to that caliber as well.

Get Comfortable with Emotional Impact

Before anything else, a leader must be comfortable facing the emotional side of themselves; otherwise, resistance floods in, and a culture of leading with fear arises. When a leader is only focused on tasks, data, and results, employees begin to feel unappreciated, become machine-like, and are always looking around the corner in fear of losing their job. Now, being "emotional" does not always mean showing weakness or shortcomings. On the contrary, utilizing emotional intelligence— being aware of, controlling, and expressing your emotions—is a strength on a deeper level. Positive emotions are developed by tapping into those feelings to confront/combat the chatter in our head and the fear of failure, and to give space to creativity.

It is the professional that can balance achievement with trust, results with optimism, and growth with grace.

Not only do great leaders understand their personal emotional impact, but they also understand that people want to work at an organization that has a *social* impact. For example, Blake Mycoskie, Founder and Chief Shoe Giver of TOMS, created a simple yet generous business plan and trademarked the One for One® for the Children of Argentina. And the results are extraordinary! TOMS Shoes has provided over

86 million pairs of shoes to children since 2006, and TOMS Eyewear has restored sight to over 600,000 people since 2011.

Every organization does not need to donate products; however, as a leader, you have a distinct ability to touch people's hearts and minds and to provide those working under you with motivation and hope that each day working will make a difference. Yes, this is a result of your do/say ratio and allows your leadership language to tell your story and make it meaningful. So, my question is this: What are you willing to learn to be an extraordinary leader who serves those who report to you? What are you willing to express to inspire your team to be its best?

Commitment to Diversity and Trust

Just as music is diverse, with many different genres, sounds, and languages, so should your boardroom be. While each instrument brings a different sound, vibration, and design, each instrument also has a job to do. Thus, as the leader/conductor, it is your job to direct the different "instruments" while protecting their unique sounds. As long as everyone is willing to learn, listen, fine-tune, and be heard, the team can play in harmony to drive results and attain goals.

Diversity is what creates harmony within the music of a company, and that sound is expressed to the customer by continuity, brand awareness, integrity of the company, and trustworthiness. When the company is synergetic and in harmony, the fans (customers) will perceive their experience as authentic. Customers will then feel seen and heard as individuals.

When customers experience this authenticity, they are more likely to engage and stay.

Perhaps at the core, it is trust that is being created amongst customers, and trust starts with the frontlines: the customer-facing employees. They are the ones we need to make sure are included in the band, as they are most visible and need to be seen as trustworthy. With that, it all starts with the leadership—the conductor.

My son is 29 years old and a bioengineer. He worked several odd jobs during high school and college to earn some extra money and help pay for his college tuition. When I was thinking through the value of an experience as it relates to trust, he was the first person I thought of.

In high school, he worked at the local cinema cleaning theaters after each showing. Gifted with a logical and tactical mind, he would always remind me that when people buy tickets for a concert, show, or movie, three truths are in play:

1. The event is going to happen.
2. It will be a positive experience.
3. If that experience turns negative, it will get messy.

I told him that I understood where he was coming from but that people want more than just a positive experience. They want an experience that will blow them away. One that will touch their mind, heart, and soul. And they trust that they will at least get the value that they paid.

Putting his logical mind to use, he told me that value is subjective, and expectations are different for each person.

And after a moment of consideration, I realized he was right. Again! Since value is subjective, it is the responsibility of the event planners to bring their very best, knowing the event will affect people in many different ways. However, it is also the responsibility of the patrons to show up as their whole selves to the experience—bringing only an expectation is taking a chance to be disappointed. By bringing their whole self, they have an opportunity to show kindness and grace, two Side B Behaviors. So, if things get messy, as they often do, they bring with them a compassion to understand.

As a leader, you need to ensure that your customers, employees, and partners have full trust and confidence in what you are doing and your commitment to doing your very best by them. But you also need to count on them to participate.

More on Trust

Nowadays, trust is fragile and broken easily, a far cry from decades past when one's word was their bond, and a handshake closed the sale.

Personally, I believe that trust and loyalty are the most important gifts you receive from customers, clients, co-workers, and leaders. Once that trust is broken, it will take a long time to earn it back (if you can ever truly get it back 100%).

I once had a leader that I trusted and valued with all that I am. I enjoyed learning from him, and our conversations about business and growth were positive. Then, without a moment's notice, the trust was gone. He made me feel like I was crazy, what many people today call gaslighting. He acted as if some of our conversations never existed or that he had expressed things to me that he did not. He began putting words in my mouth and then said we talked about things that never reached me or my desk. And that is when I lost complete trust in his words and actions.

My lack of trust put me on the defense, and our conversations became superficial the very few times we talked after I began to notice these problems. Why I bring this story to your attention is to illustrate that without trust, we have nothing—no differentiator, no common ground. Why else would people want to work with you, or customers/clients buy from your company?

All great leaders know that with honesty comes trust, and with trust comes loyalty.

The Bonus Track

My goal is to help people uncover their emotional legacy, discover why it is important to them, and how they can show up each day to those they serve to make a difference and achieve goals. This book is your opportunity to take a deep dive into the characteristics that are natural to us or perhaps that we learned while growing up yet didn't really sharpen when we entered the business world. We didn't focus on them because they were not really talked about as needed or important in business. Instead, we let them fizzle away. However, these are the Side B Legacy Behaviors that, as we get older, seem to circle back as we remember all that helped make the world a positive place for us to engage in. They are:

- Curiosity
- Passion
- Trustworthiness
- High Ethics
- Gratitude
- Courage
- Kindness
- Courage
- Sincerity
- Certainty

This is Side B, the silent track of leadership, which remains often unspoken for a variety of reasons. Yet, it is the true bonus track for our Authentic Leadership Legacy.

Unfortunately, oftentimes when you display these characteristics in the workforce, unless you are in HR, you might get written off as unstable, not knowing your business, or weak. However, it is just the opposite! When leaders finally realize that walking in these behaviors produces results, loyalty, and a culture of trust, people will wonder why they didn't see it before.

I believe that many leaders can behave in true service to their people; however, it is hard work. Regrettably, like anything else, sometimes the leader will give in and conform to how they think they are supposed to lead. For example, knowing all the Side A work and focus that we need, it seems easier to ignore the work it takes to show kindness, optimism, trust, and courage. After all, it takes strength to show up differently.

But it is not impossible.

I was speaking with one such leader, Meshell Baker, who makes it look easy to adopt Side B. She is the founder of Meshell Baker Enterprises, LLC, co-founder of Shift/Co, sales authentic-selling zealot, mentor at Collective Brains, and a confidence expert with wiseHER. Meshell is dedicated to building confidence around the globe, and when she speaks, she exudes optimism.

I was on a video conference call with her, and I couldn't help but notice her behavior. She was shining and spoke with such optimistic language that I had to immediately ask her to take a professional business assessment. It was not surprising that, when she did, the assessment showed that her top three Side B Legacy Behaviors were optimism, sincerity, and graciousness.

To get a clear picture of what her individual daily routine looks like as an optimistic, I asked if she would share what it is that she wakes up to every day. She reminded me of the distinction between saying "I get to do" vs. "I have to do" and lives in accordance with her optimistic attitude. She feels the world today is smothered with the "I have to dos." Many times, we are faced with a task or project that does not align with who we are, and, therefore, we get overwhelmed. In those cases, it's time to simply say no. We talked about how it is good to remove the clutter and get clarity on our vision, our unique selves. "We have been numbers-driven for so long time that people don't even know who they work for; they just have to show up for a paycheck." Leaders, this goes to show right here that our people need to see, hear, and feel your Side B gifts!

Leaders, it's time to understand your greatest potential is not in a task or program; it is in your *people*. Show up in your legacy and see what happens next. Just like Henry, this is your journey.

AUTHENTIC LEADERSHIP LEGACY: PUTTING SIDE A AND SIDE B TOGETHER

Though this might sound disheartening, hear me out. There will come a moment in your career where you get lost in doing nothing but "stuff" and shut down who you are. When that point happens, your record is now simply skipping.

And yes, this happens to just about everyone, at least those who will openly admit to it.

Why does this happen? To be very honest with you, it is because we have completed many of the tasks we set out to complete, or everything we do feels repetitive. As extraordinary humans and leaders, we are always searching to grow, learn, write our own stories, and become the best we can be. By putting your Side A and Side B together, you begin to remix your style, choose what you want from each side, and balance those skills to achieve the very best results you can for your team, your family, and, ultimately, yourself. You become a balanced leader, one who is not willing to conform but leans into their emotional side as well.

When you do, you begin to feel again and will be forever grateful and humbled. This is the starting point of learning Authentic Leadership Legacy and genuinely serving others before yourself.

Close the Gap: When Leaders Grow, Results Follow

We've all likely heard of the Alpha Male, the Boys' Club, or even the "Locker-Room" mentality. However, this mentality doesn't just apply to males; it is for females as well. I have seen a great deal of female leaders who are strongly spirited in their own rights. Seeing more women in leadership roles and c-suite positions is excellent, but we still have work to do to close the gender gap even further. I am not afraid to say that female leaders, for many reasons, do not get the same training or coaching as male ones. I've seen it across corporate America, in entertainment, sports, and other fields. Yes, women are becoming more confident and respected for their individuality, but a gap of inequality remains.

That said, I am proud to say I am an Alpha Commander—a personality with the ability to produce strong results. Like a few of my male counterparts, I enjoy driving results and challenges and invest a lot of energy in making the impossible happen. However, I do not often exude the "big presence" that others expect of leaders. So, the question you may be asking yourself is this: Is there really that much of a difference between male and female leadership?

Yes and no. When given the opportunity to lead, a good portion of the time, women are already labeled and need to prove what they are *not* as leaders, rather than what they *are*. This scenario is quite different for men. However, on the other hand, a majority of women have a good grasp on how to lead with emotion yet also with discipline and account-ability, a combination which, in today's environment, is important.

When we all advocate for each other to be our best, then, as leaders, we get the best from our people, and results naturally follow. I had the opportunity to speak with two of my favor-ite leaders, Tim Rubert, VP of Sales of Bound Tree Medical and retired United States Coast Guard Officer, and Lauren Bailey, Founder and CEO of Factor 8 and #GirlsClub. We first discussed the qualities and mindsets of leadership, asking when leaders function at their best.

"What are the attributes of great leadership, in your opinion?"

- *Tim: Honesty, integrity, passion, and communication.*
- *Lauren: Encouragement, accountability, confidence, and communication.*

Tim went on to add more: "At the very top of the list, it must be honesty and integrity. Because if you do not have those, it makes it difficult to make tough decisions and have your teams listen to you. As a leader, you are going to make not necessarily popular decisions, whether it's a compensa-tion plan, downsizing, or even putting a great employee on a performance plan. There is no way to do that if you do not have honesty and integrity. Once you have that, you must be able to show passion for the job. When people understand you are passionate about what you are doing, then you are communicating with the team and letting them know what's going on and not be afraid to do it yourself. I will not ask someone to do something I would not be willing to do myself."

Lauren says the magic buttons for most sellers (especially women) are encouragement and confidence. What companies can do to encourage more women into leadership is to not just post the job but go to a woman they believe in and encourage her to apply for the job. This is an incredibly powerful action that has no real downside. The best thing that happens is you have just changed somebody's entire life. The worst thing that happens is you made their day!

"What are some of the differences between men and women leaders?"

- *Tim: I think there are some differences. I do not think they are extensive.*

- *Lauren: It's more about perception. Men don't fight the "B" label or the "nurturing mother" label like women do.*

Tim believes it has more to do with your life experiences, not whether you are male or female. There are a lot of female business leaders, including in the military and Congress. Of course, as a leader himself, he did not want to stereotype, but he thinks women might have more compassion than men and adds, "It's not right or wrong, good or bad. It's just a trait."

Lauren adds that we are starting to see that change. She does hear women pegged as serial nurturers more than men, but honestly, has seen women sales leaders who are tough as nails and men who tend to be like den mothers. More importantly, in the end, it comes down to results and accountability. If you are not tough enough to hold people accountable, then it is hard to overcome that whether you are a man *or* a woman. She believes, as there are now more women leaders at all points on the spectrum, we will see the gap close. In the future, people will be labeled simply as "leaders" instead of "women leaders." COVID-19 also helped everyone focus more on empathy and kindness, and we are going to find the need for the balance between being results-focused and people-focused. We are going to need more empathetic, results-driven leaders to keep our people around longer.

"What is your 'must do' leadership tip?"

- *Tim: Leadership, in a very decisive way, is having the courage to make the decisions and the confidence to execute those decisions.*

- *Lauren: Execute with confidence, and results will occur with the people you serve; therefore, serve them well and enjoy the ride.*

Both Tim and Lauren are avid music fans and understand that music is a bit like leadership storytelling—there is a beginning, middle, and end, which are the results. Sometimes singing the same old song can become tedious, and, as a leader, you need to know when it's time to turn on the radio and create new music using the same instruments!

WHAT DOES YOUR AUTHENTIC LEADERSHIP LEGACY LOOK LIKE NOW?

Think about who you turn to for deep conversations. Most people would say that it is their family, friends, religious leaders, or healthcare workers. Yet, we spend 8-10 hours a day at work, leading people and getting the job done, listening to others gossip, tossing responsibilities over the wall, hearing stories of what is wrong, complaining, and throwing in a few celebrations.

Does that sound like most jobs or places of employment? Maybe to some that is not the case; however, I hear that it is more often than not. Why is that? Is it because people who are on the front lines feel it is a job rather than a career?

I think about this distinction a lot. When does a job become a career, with promotions or a title? This is another area waiting for a remix! Those leaders who embrace their Side B Behaviors allow everyone to feel that the work they do is a career, a journey, an essential part of the team. If we can reframe this perception to our people, our people will reframe their workplace conversations, and we get to live out our Side B Legacy Behaviors.

We should feed our desire to learn and lead people, not just concern ourselves with data and numbers. When you can positively change the work environment or culture in any way, you become the next "Hound Dog" by Elvis or "Maggie May" by Rod Stewart, or even "You Can't Always Get What You Want" by the Rolling Stones (all Side B songs that became great hits in their own right, by the way).

Why is the remix so valuable? Often, it is what we don't know that we are missing in our leadership, that inner strength that is needed to truly serve people and find joy within ourselves. As leaders, we need to find our own path by trial and error. We need to understand what will make us fly. It is neither Side A nor Side B skills alone that make us extraordinary leaders; instead, we need a mix of both.

Our highly valued Side A skills are what we strive for to win, get results, and succeed in our careers. On the other hand, Side B Behaviors are necessary for our compassion to impact those around us, including family. By balancing these skills and behaviors, we have the courage to show ourselves to others, something that is needed in our world today.

When you are thriving at that level of leadership, you are achieving and impacting, you are serving your people, and you are willing to step into your positive emotional behavior. It is within that remix of your leadership style, adding both Side A and Side B, that you begin to leave a positive Authentic Leadership Legacy.

My recommendation is to not be afraid to achieve great results while simultaneously embracing those emotional conversations. Side B allows you to be emotionally attuned to others' feelings and allows people to feel important and valued. Side B gives you that language. Have the courage to remix your playlist and serve people with a balance of both hard and soft skills, and they, in turn, will bring their best every day.

Song: "Her Song"
She knows how to complete her mission.
Achieves her goals with passion, not position.
She'll go the distance, and it won't be long.
'Til everyone is singing her song.

Lyrics by Paula White

CHAPTER 5

THE SIDE B LEGACY BAND

"I think any time I've ever got down or ever felt low
the one thing that picks me up from that
is writing a song about it. At least you've got
a positive experience out of a bad experience."
—*Singer Ed Sheeran*

After his conversation with Pat and Clint, Henry closes his door and sits down to catch a glimpse of his dark reflection on the idle monitor screen. With the song "Look for the Good" by Jason Mraz playing in the background, he truthfully looks at himself for the first time in a long while. Frustration, anger, sadness, and guilt are all staring back at him. Henry finds himself holding his breath with each question he writes down.

1. Why can't I find one solid week for a family vacation?

2. Do I lead with a culture of fear?

3. Why couldn't Pat tell me what was happening or how I could help?

4. Have I become so busy that I have forgotten my core leadership values?

5. Do people only tell me what I want to hear?

6. Do I serve up or down?

7. If I get hit by a truck tomorrow, what's the plan?

8. Where am I now, and what is important to me?

Henry decides to leave early that evening, take this list, and have a conversation with his wife—his partner in life—and sit in the discomfort. This is not a time to make any rash decisions. As he hops in the car, he sits for a moment and turns on the radio, hoping to get an answer.

And what is playing? "Werewolves of London" by Warren Zevon. Henry just bursts out in laughter. He can't stop laughing, remembering the theater class in his senior year in high school. The year-end project was to perform a five-minute skit based on a song. Most students chose a song from musicals like *Grease*, *Cats*, or *Little Shop of Horrors*. Some chose popular songs like "Thriller" by Michael Jackson or "Walk Like an Egyptian" by the Bangles. As for Henry's group, well, they chose "Werewolves of London"—the very song he was listening to.

He arrives home, still thinking of that night on stage, walking out dressed as the werewolf, holding a Chinese menu in his hand. Though he isn't sure why he finds this so funny at the moment, he does. However, it doesn't last. The frustration and anger creep back in, the black cloud returning as he pulls into the driveway.

Later that evening, after the firestorm inside him subsides and the glimmer of hope appears following his conversation with his wife, Henry books a flight to St. John U.S.V.I. and adds that song on a playlist to give himself courage for difficult conversations. They had both shed more than a few tears. But as the truth emerged, they shared their bottled-up feelings, their tears washing away much of their pain, leaving the path ahead clearer.

♪♪♪

When are leaders born? Is it when you fall and get back up? Is it when you finally put others first? Or is it when you realize that leadership is all about the people you serve? I know my leadership was born after the loss of a team, and I flipped the organizational chart. Like Henry, our minds first become cluttered with stories of self-doubt, thinking about conversations and successes/failures. When the mind is working in overdrive, heading for a cliff, and we are crying out for that moment of clarity, that is when a leader is born. We begin to search and look for answers from those we trust using our list of questions.

Dobie Gray has a song titled "Drift Away" that talks about slowing down and going for a simple drive, and allowing the music to heal you. When you are ready to sit in your darkness peacefully, that list of questions and answers will come as you allow your heart and mind to see your Side B Legacy. Trust me, at this time, no one ever feels like anyone else would understand; however, if you open up, find your courage, and become vulnerable, you will find so many stories within you to share with your network of professionals and friends that believe in you!

We are now seeing Henry's transformation. He turned the record over and started thinking about how to lead with emotion and what that would mean for everyone at the company. I have seen this type of transformation time and time again, and it is extraordinary if it is done authentically and comes from the heart. The Side B leadership style cannot be faked, and it cannot be shortsighted or temporary. But when transformation happens, get ready to celebrate!

OPPORTUNITY FOR CHANGE

It is now time for you to understand that your Legacy Behavior starts with an open door and trust. It is with authentic communication and trust that your teams begin to believe in you and want to break through walls for you and the company. People are our number-one investment, and when we believe in them authentically, there is no greater reward (*except* for all the productivity and success that will naturally occur). Then you get to trust that what is being *said* is being *done* by both your employees and, more importantly, yourself. There is a strategic balance between results, execution, and behavior. This is your opportunity to make a tremendous difference in today's work environment.

Over and over, I was asked the same question by my leadership team.

"What's the secret sauce to achieving goals?"

There is no recipe or secret sauce per se, but it does boil down to this simple truth: You get more from people when they know you have their back and are intentional about getting to know them on a personal level. During the first week of onboarding, I would ask each new hire to write down and share, if they are comfortable, both a professional and personal goal and their favorite band, song, or genre. This exercise gave me the opportunity to personally identify with people. I even had a greater chance to help them to not only achieve their goals but also visualize them by understanding what drives them to achieve, and what success looks like in their eyes. As a visionary myself, I was able to see things happening in the future and could outline what it would take to achieve that goal for each employee.

Now, I want to come back to some of the questions we asked at the beginning of this book as we were talking about legacy. What do you want to be remembered for? Let's take it a step further: What is your theme song? What is your playlist?

Do you want to be remembered for all your achievements, or do you want to be remembered for extraordinary leadership, recognized for your accomplishments *and* the way you treated, empowered, and cared for people? By way of reminder, the following traits are what people look for in a leader: kindness, passion, trustworthiness, curiosity, graciousness, sincerity, certainty, optimism, high ethics, and courage. These traits will show up differently in each person, and everyone brings a unique strength and individuality to the leadership table.

When you're bringing those unique strengths to the workplace and your team, not only are you bringing diversity of thought to the table, but your efforts will have a positive impact on results. It's important for your people to think differently, understand that it is okay for them to discuss and be proud of their emotional strengths, and not fear they will be held back for it. Do you think a band member would get kicked out of the band for playing a different instrument? No, that is what adds a special sound and creates a full song.

And now, without further ado… are you ready to meet the band? Those silent musicians waiting to make their appearance inside you?

Here we go!

THE DRUMMER: CURIOUS

I would like to first introduce you to the **Drummer**, or the **Curious Legacy Behavior**. If you are the drummer, you are a

visionary—a forward thinker who is the heartbeat of the company. You are always interested in plotting the path to the best future for the company, and you keep the tempo by seeking out ways to find opportunities for growth and progress. As the drummer, you are consistently looking for answers to the many questions rolling around in your head. And when at their best, drummers have a grasp of what is happening within the organization from ceiling to floor, much like a drummer in a band knows what each instrument is playing.

Those leading with a Curious Legacy Behavior always ask questions about what can be improved or what others see, especially those on the "floor." The drummer knows that they likely have great ideas because they are closer to the customer. And as a result, the people you serve will feel empowered and will likely remain loyal, which will increase productivity.

If your Legacy Behavior is curiosity, you are fortunate to inspire many people to believe in themselves. You will be remembered for the lunches, the one-on-ones, the time you took to ask questions and truly listen. You will continue to keep the tempo for your company and ensure everyone is marching forward to the same beat. I am honored to know you!

♪♪♪

"One good thing about music,
when it hits you, you feel no pain."
—*Bob Marley*

There was a time in my career that I particularly enjoyed (and had the passion for) building and executing. I relied heavily on creating, innovating, and strategically aligning corporate initiatives and results to build a team, and I was in my element. The 30,000-foot view was my sweet spot, although I felt limited in conversations. When I spoke with other leaders, many didn't understand my thought process or didn't have experience in my area of the business world.

Still, I absolutely loved what I was doing, and it became a part of my identity. I would research, ask questions, and analyze all options to ensure I was creating a best-in-class environment for the team and a best-in-class team for company results. Now, the one thing I could do was create the idea; however, I had difficulty presenting it to the executive team and hoped someone else would share on my behalf.

On a side note: It really wasn't until recently
I was able to find my voice,
although I had to tame it a bit. #self-awareness

One afternoon, I remember sitting in my office and working on a plan to continue to build and expand our sales department. When I looked up as I was in mid-thought, I noticed one of our executive leaders standing at the door. He asked if I would go to lunch, and as a manager/employee at the time, I was thrilled about the opportunity (although a bit nervous). In my head, all sorts of questions popped up in a matter of moments.

Why me? Why lunch? What did he want to talk about? What could I possibly help him with?

He probably noticed my angst, even as I tried to be still. I could hardly speak as we walked to Boston Market, engaging in small talk along the way. When we arrived, we ordered lunch and sat down. It was a beautiful day and the restaurant was empty. It was a very relaxed lunch, and it turns out that all he genuinely wanted was to ask a few questions about growing the sales region I was responsible for at the time.

I probably spoke most of the time because, as a drummer, he was curious and honestly wanted to help me to create and bring new ideas to the conversation. From that point on, I felt extremely comfortable talking to him, and we would meet often.

To this day, I appreciate his curiosity, vision, and willingness to experiment with ideas.

How can you spot the **Drummer** behaving in their **Curious Legacy**?

1. "Responsibility with curiosity" is their motto.

2. They ask a lot of questions and like to see things from a different perspective to move forward.

3. Every conversation starts with a question, and they sit back and listen for an answer. The key here is that they are actively listening, making sure not to make any judgments.

4. They take time to wonder, read, and figure out strategies.

5. They speak less and listen intentionally, looking to have all their team seen and heard.

THE LEAD GUITARIST: PASSIONATE

Next, I would like to introduce the **Lead Guitarist**, or the **Passionate Legacy Behavior**. If you are the lead guitarist, your

legacy is incredibly special. By nature, you hold people accountable and drive results. It is your responsibility to nail the song structure, and your genuine passion is contagious. People want to work for and hear you as the lead guitarist because you fill in the gaps and lead them through challenging times with genuine grace and leadership. It may not be easy for you or the team, but your employees will walk with you and challenge themselves to meet your passion.

If you are a lead guitarist, I implore you to be proud of your legacy and know that what you bring to the table is extraordinary. However, there are a few things you need to be cautious of when talking about accountability. One, when holding others accountable, strive for the highest level of accountability for everyone because allowing for a low level of accountability for some will only lead to frustration and gossip. Two, as a passionate person, keep it positive and try not to fill any gaps with negativity when you, yourself, may be frustrated. After all, we all have our moments. Three, you must remain positive in your passionate legacy and be driven by your positive emotions to achieve extraordinary results. If you don't, your legacy is playing the song in the wrong key, unable to hold people accountable.

We count on you to make our day rich and productive, and if you're involved, we know a difference was made in the world today.

♪♪♪

"To achieve great things, two things are needed;
a plan, and not quite enough time."
—*Leonard Bernstein*

When I was researching passionate behavior, many leaders came to mind; however, one person stood out: Anneke Seley, founder and managing partner of Reality Works Group and co-author of *Sales 2.0* and *Next Era Selling*. She honestly believes that people are the prerequisite to results, and as a leader, she is enthusiastic to serve her employees.

When I asked what drives her, Anneke responded, "I am a competitive perfectionist that likes to help people and change things for the better." Her passion certainly shines through all she does, running a diverse, virtual next-generation sales consulting company and working with smart, creative people who are fun to work with and open to experimenting with new ideas. She is passionate about putting the right teams together, having an impact on others, being innovative, intellectually stimulating, and producing great results.

She is passionate about taking responsibility for results and building an enthusiastic organization. So, I asked Anneke when leaders in this Legacy Behavior serve their team best. This was her response:

- When they are fully present and open to new ideas.

- When they do not jump to conclusions and make assumptions about what others need.

- When they help with creative brainstorming.

- When they ask, "What are your thoughts on how I can best help or serve you?"

Anneke is not only someone I admire, but the passion in her heart and legacy will drive results all day long.

How can you spot the **Lead Guitarist** behaving in their **Passionate Legacy**?

1. "Taking initiative with passion" is their motto.

2. They help others grow and understand what it takes to get the results by working *with* them, not just telling them what to do.

3. They exude a positive energy for people and the work they do.

4. They stand in their genuine self, filling gaps with a reflection of what could be.

5. They have a competitive edge and take care of the business and its people.

THE BASS GUITARIST: ETHICAL

I would now like to introduce the **Bass Guitarist**, or the **Ethical Legacy Behavior**. What an important legacy to leave! If you lead with this Legacy Behavior, you are an exceptional communicator, deep in integrity, and rich in unique sound. When you speak, you can be sure you are heard. It's a little Stevie Ray Vaughan action at its best. We believe in you, ethical leader, and the integrity to communicate the truth is the greatest gift you give to the world. People know you speak the truth and are noticeably clear and direct in communication. You are truly the backbone of a band but hardly get recognized. *I see you!*

Having baseline integrity is one thing, but even in those small moments where you could slip in a little white lie or discourage something for another's benefit, you don't! You serve people with a command of your ethics and expect the same from everyone else.

This is probably the rarest Legacy to lead with, but it can be done with your head held high. You are a bright spot in the organization. You are the Bass Guitarist.

♪♪♪

"Music has always been used as the gateway
for change and conversation."
—*Kitty Cash*

I have worked with two phenomenal ethical leaders: one at a time in my life that was full of growth, and the other for a very short time. They probably don't even know that I have included them in this book, let alone this section! Showing up in the Ethical Legacy Behavior is exceedingly rare, and to have been led by two in my career has been incredibly rewarding.

The first leader is like a brother to me. He has guided my path for many years, and I can tell you that, without hesitation, his clients trusted him because of his integrity. He always supported authentic communication and was very respectful to all people he met, whether friend, foe, or stranger.

I can recall a specific time he wanted to talk to me about my work. I had just had my second child, and I really wanted to be home with my kids. He could sense my tension and called me into his office. "How can we get you home?" he asked—simple as that. He even helped me figure out the budget! A leader who can serve their people with honest communication gains respect and loyalty.

This second leader is one I continue to learn a great deal from. He is unpretentious, kind, and holds high expectations of himself and others. He is cause-motivated and came from one of the most admired careers, firefighting/EMS. His balance of being straightforward and thoughtful has earned him the trust of many. The company, team, and customers that surround him hold him in high esteem. He works extremely hard to take care of each.

I remember sitting in his office one day, looking to implement a new direction for our department. He respected the idea and said he would take it to the board of directors, and because of his ethical behavior, I believed he would do what he said. And he did. He also came back to me and advised they had already moved in a different direction. What I want you to see is that there was no pretending, hiding behind a curtain, or blaming. He got the answer and came back to me immediately with the decision. Shortly after, he decided to retire. He has certainly left a legacy to always do the right thing, even if it hurts.

How can you spot the **Bass Guitarist** behaving in their **Ethical Legacy**?

1. "Execution with engagement" is their motto.
2. The legacy they leave by being ethical is unassuming and rich.
3. They are unpretentious, kind, and have high expectations.
4. They have an incredible do/say ratio.
5. They make no assumptions to dilute the truth.

THE PIANIST: SINCERE

I would like to introduce you to **the Pianist,** or the **Sincere Legacy Behavior**.

 The pianist seems to be strong in many paradoxical traits and has the balance of both left and right brain. They can show discipline and yet be easygoing. If you lead with this Legacy Behavior, you likely have the gift of sincerity—meaning your support of others is genuine and always done in good faith. You will be remembered for being honest with how you act and who you are as a leader.

If you recall, the pianist's primary role is twofold: to either stand out *or* provide support to a song. In either scenario, they are sincere and heartfelt, providing both harmony and melody, or decision-making and conflict resolution.

If your Legacy Behavior is sincerity, I want to honor you and your willingness to show up just as you are. We see you taking the lead role when necessary and taking the backseat for others to lead when the scenario calls for it.

♪♪♪

"One of the best ways to relate
is giving them something musically."
—*Trinidad James*

I recently had the opportunity to speak with Sandra Leigh Stosz, retired United States Coast Guard Vice Admiral, about her experiences and work with the USCG. Not only is she an amazing leader, but she has also worked her entire adult life in service of others. We talked about what it means to leave a legacy. She and I both agreed that it is not up to the leader to work towards leaving a legacy, so to speak, but that showing up daily with positive behavior is impactful to the people you serve.

Sandy was accepted into the United States Coast Guard Academy at the age of 18 and, in her words, "never looked back." Being the third class of women accepted into the service academy at the time, women only represented 5% of the total class cadet count. She told me that being in the minority was incredibly challenging. A lot of men still thought women should not be there and made it difficult for them to make their way through the good and bad—just like in life. However, Sandy told me that for every classmate who didn't think she should be there or ignored her, there were four or five who were friendly and supported her, so it balanced out.

Those leaders with the Sincere Legacy Behavior trait show strength in making decisions. Sandy talked to me about her discovery of three decision impediments that kill the decision-making process. They are:

1. Analysis Paralysis: Needing to have 100% of the facts and information before deciding.

2. The Consensus Conundrum: Looking for 100% agreement.

3. The "Being Nice" Illusion: Making decisions based on making others happy.

The key to this legacy is that decision is followed by the willingness to take *responsibility* for that decision. In her career, Sandy has been faced with many complicated, not-so-popular decisions that eventually landed on her desk.

Sandy only looked to do her best—to give as much as she could, both personally and professionally.

Sandy is a true leader who understands that legacy cannot be personally created or be self-serving; instead, your legacy is ultimately determined by the people you serve.

How can you spot the **Pianist** behaving in their **Sincere Legacy**?

1. "Discipline with sincerity" is their motto.

2. They are decisive in their decision-making approach to ensure it is inclusive and will benefit the company as well as the people working there.

3. They handle conflict well and ensure that there is harmony amongst the group.

4. Their decisions are based on risk and sincerity, not greed.

5. Most importantly, having balance is essential to them.

THE RHYTHM GUITARIST: TRUSTWORTHY

I would now like to introduce the **Rhythm Guitarist** or the **Trustworthy Legacy Behavior**. The Rhythm Guitar is a powerful instrument, and its primary role is collaboration and, of course, rhythm. This is usually the sound that can provide motivation and trust, which, in the context of business and music, can accomplish a significant amount. Leading from this Legacy Behavior of trustworthiness is an immensely powerful legacy to serve people.

If you lead from the Trustworthy Legacy Behavior, you trust your team to move the needle for the company, and the team trusts you to help. As the people who work for you, we will walk through walls and stand by you during any negative discussions at the watercooler. Your corporate walk will be challenging if there is a lack of trust, as you do not want people to only be agreeable—you also want to be challenged. You know it is your responsibility to trust and be trusted.

Leading from the trustworthy legacy, you make the most difference in a person's life and career. Trust me.

♪♪♪

"Until you're ready to look foolish,
you'll never have the possibility of being great."
—*Cher*

My grandfather, whom I called Pop, was an incredible, strong, and compassionate leader. He had a very successful career with Lazarus department stores as vice president of procurement and sales. Lazarus was a retail store in Columbus, Ohio, which was a part of Federated Department Stores (we used to watch the stock quotes in the paper together). Now, this chain is called Macy's.

Pop, a devoted and loyal employee by nature, was a 6'2" man who played for the Portsmouth Spartans (who eventually moved to Detroit to become the Detroit Lions). He was a big man on the outside with a heart of gold on the inside.

As I was growing up, I would ask him to tell me his story about the scarves again. As reluctant as he may have been to discuss it, he always made it a lesson in trusting your gut, people, and sense of adventure.

The year was about 1952, and fashion trends seemed to be finding their way to America by way of Europe. So Pop, being Pop, hopped on a plane and landed in London with several bottles of whiskey and Scotch and a budget to bring a new trend back to Lazarus in Columbus, Ohio.

After landing in London, he took the train to Paris. Now, Pop was a man of his word and enjoyed talking to other people. In the dining car, he sat at a large table, looking for others to join him. People would come and go, and he would listen to their stories. Then a gentleman and his wife sat down, and she was wearing a beautiful silk scarf. He knew right then what he had to bring back to Mr. Lazarus. As they began talking, he discovered that silk scarves were the hot item that everyone wanted in Europe. So, naturally, he began to ask where he could purchase them, and the gentleman told him that they were a luxury item and only certain stores carried the beautiful scarves. Pop explained why he was on his way to Paris and offered the gentleman and his wife a bottle of American whiskey for the scarf she was wearing. They agreed.

As they were pulling into Paris, he knew his goal was to get his hands on as many silk scarves as possible. He was going to spend the whole budget, and, in those days, that was a risk he was willing to take. Although nervous, he proceeded ahead. Scarves couldn't be found in places like Columbus, Ohio. Maybe New York, Chicago, and Los Angeles, but not Columbus!

What would Mr. Lazarus think, say, and do if it was a flop? he worried. But he ultimately trusted his gut and decided to go all in, purchasing as much as he could with his budget. However, that did not seem good enough, so he pulled out the Scotch and whiskey, and the trading began. Pop always loved a good challenge, and upon his return, the marketing was completed, and the rollout of the scarves began. Pop stood behind the wall and watched the scarves being laid out on the center table in the aisleway, proud of his work. And it paid off.

It only took one day for the scarves to completely sell out.

This was not the first nor the last time the Lazarus family put their trust in him (although this one made them more nervous than any other!). In fact, they trusted him so much that after his purchase, Mr. Lazarus sent both Grandmother and Pop to the Lazarus home in Florida for a month! I mean, who does that anymore?! And from that time forward, Pop would build that same kind of trust with his team—trust based on results, achievement, collaboration, and challenges. Great leaders in a Trustworthy Legacy believe in their teams, give them wings to fly, and when they see signs of stress, anxiousness, or burnout, they give them room to breathe.

Ten years after his retirement from Lazarus, they "roasted" Pop, and the scarf story was one of the first ones told.

How can you spot the **Rhythm Guitarist** behaving in their **Trustworthy Legacy**?

1. "Strategic achievement with trust" is their motto.

2. They enjoy difficult tasks and collaborate with others.

3. They genuinely believe that it is necessary to look at what is in the best interest of the people they serve.

4. They know the difference between blind trust and truth and expect it in return.

5. They motivate people by actions, not just words.

THE VOCALIST: OPTIMISTIC

I would next like to introduce you to the **Vocalist,** or the **Optimistic Legacy Behavior**. If you lead with an Optimistic Legacy, you are the frontman/woman of the band. You command the room, empowering others to come on your journey of positivity while providing clarity and direction. You are hopeful and optimistic about the future, and like the frontman/woman, you will tell us how it is in a frank and positive manner.

Leading with an Optimistic Legacy is contagious. However, you must be sure you are not leading with blind optimism. Yes, your team has problems to overcome and solutions to provide, but in your eyes, they can accomplish it all. Optimism is a behavior that may become extinct if we don't learn how to cultivate it for our future. You know, that "I accomplish anything I set my heart to" attitude that today seems to be getting lost amongst the growing technology stacks and the fear of losing careers. I count on us, the Optimistic Legacy, to help cultivate a new generation of positive optimism for being ourselves and accomplishing our goals. People need to feel valued to be positive. Will you help me?

If you lead from the Optimistic Legacy, as the frontman/woman, your voice should be heard loud and clear as you empower all to see possibilities for the future.

♪♪♪

"Musicians want to be the loud voice
for so many quiet hearts."
—*Billy Joel*

As a manager of a growing inside sales team, in 2013, I had the opportunity to attend the AA-ISP Leadership Summit. This is where I first met Bob Perkins, founder of AA-ISP and a songwriter/musician. Bob showed up onstage wearing a plaid jacket and jeans, and he was inspiring and optimistic about the direction of inside sales.

Early on in his career, he led a field sales team and then got into this thing called "telesales." He said, "Within a year, I literally fell in love with telesales/inside sales." He was not exactly sure why but thought it was because telesales was considered the underdog team.

Like most who lead with the Optimistic Behavior Legacy, Bob was self-motivated and on a mission to prove that inside sales could sell as effectively as in the field—and not just simple transactional sales, but bigger complex things as well. Bob continued to build inside sales teams for many organizations. Along the way, he became more curious about what others were doing in this field and what he could do to help. He wanted to provide direction and clarity for growth. Being a student, he began to compare notes and work with other companies with their inside sales leaders, asking them questions like "How do you motivate your team?" and "How do you compensate your people?"

Bob was a sponge.

This is precisely when Bob got the idea for an association. He says, "As I began to share that knowledge, it became noticeably clear that there wasn't any type of training. There was no place that we could come together to learn from each other. This is where the idea of an association started. I talked about it for four years and kept coming back to it. So, I called a good friend, Larry, and shared my idea with him. At the time, it was only to have one conference a year. Now, it has grown into several conferences, online training, workshops, and a community of like-minded individuals to connect with and help each other. Now, look where it is today! I never even dreamed we would have chapters around the world!"

Bob feels it is the leader's job to enrich and develop the lives of others. "Leadership is about inspiring others to achieve great things and to be their best," he says. "There is nothing more satisfying than watching people improve and advance in their careers and accomplish great things. To be motivated is the most beautiful thing in the world, and to lead a team that is highly motivated and has such high expectations that they could run through walls, you know, believing there is no obstacle to greatness, is awesome!"

Bob lives by the motto "Others first; self last." I agree, and often, I see the opposite from leaders. That is one of the biggest mistakes new leaders make. I know; remember when I told you I was a "keep your head down and let results speak for you" leader? That was my biggest mistake early in my career. Now, when Bob gets up on that stage, he empowers others to serve people, drive results, and look toward the future.

But I feel I must be clear about something: Leading with optimism does *not* mean being happy-go-lucky, blindly positive, and afraid to make tough decisions. In fact, it is just the opposite. The optimistic leader is enthusiastic about goal attainment, knows what to do to act in alignment with the business, and creates a vision for people to feel trusted—even if it's uncomfortable. And even if it's less than positive at first!

"Great leaders put themselves out there and are transparent and people-first. That does not mean you are not going to have a tough conversation. As a people-first leader, you must have hard talks, and you are going to call people out on the carpet. It is not pleasant. You will not like doing it. But you've got to remember, you work for your team as a whole and must provide clarity and direction," Bob says.

How can you spot the **Vocalist** behaving in their **Optimistic Legacy**?

1. "Remarkable results with optimism" is their motto.
2. They are genuinely happy, often with a smile on their face.
3. They honestly believe people can accomplish anything they set their minds to.
4. "I can't" is not in their vocabulary.
5. They are self-motivated and believe everyone else is as well.

EVERY PERSON LEAVES A LEGACY

Every day, you *get to* step into your leadership role and leave a legacy for those you serve. Good or bad, it's ultimately up to you. I had someone tell me recently that there is an art to getting out of your own way, and I believe music can help you do just that to step into creativity and focus. Listen for the music that speaks to you, the music that helps your mindset, your musical mindset. Each leader is unique and brings their own set of behavioral values to leading. What is yours? Is it "your" time to pivot, remix, and uncover your path? Choose YOU!

Song: "There You Are"
Every person leaves a legacy
For better or worse.
You get to choose if
It is a blessing or curse.

Lyrics by Paula White

CHAPTER 6

SIDE B BAND: CHOOSE YOUR MUSIC

"We need leaders who get to be
'whole life perspective' leaders in their roles."
—*Melinda French Gates*

After Henry's thoughtful questions and conversation with his wife, he begins to become aware of his unique leadership style, which includes his Side B Legacy Behaviors. He knows this is an area for needed growth and begins by defining two areas where he can improve.

One, he wants to be more intentional with his frontline people by asking questions, learning about things like what they are hearing from their customers and what drives them to come to work each day. Two, he wants to purposefully create a space for diversity of thought by picking two employee representatives from each department—without seeing their names, to avoid unintentional bias—to have a quarterly lunch to brainstorm on market ideas, better understand the current corporate culture, and get to know more people on an individual level. These lunches will make room for creativity and groundbreaking ideas, he believes.

Henry knows the key for both of these areas is to start with some lighthearted music and stay open to all ideas, allowing for thoughts to flow without judgment. He adds these two objectives to his already busy calendar, knowing he must create his own space to do the work he already has to do. However, now Henry appreciates the peace and motivation that occurs when the music plays, and he is able to accomplish his tasks and work and make decisions with the well-deserved time and dedicated attention they require.

He is beginning to learn that when music aligns with the proper mindset, it provides clarity, focus, and creativity to accomplish his goals. Henry also has his "one song" ready to be heard at any given moment throughout the day to help him be an extraordinary leader to the people he serves. He is enthusiastic about showing up and developing his Side B

Behavioral skills to engage with as many people as he can within the company to bring a better perspective (not just assumptions) to the company leaders and board members.

He begins to plan for his day by creating a Leadership

Playlist for his drive to work, starting with American Authors' "Best Day of My Life," immediately followed by The Black Eyed Peas' "I Gotta Feeling." Both songs play just long enough for him to back out of his driveway, drive to the office, and pull into the company's parking lot.

Henry is now ready to embrace any day with a musical mindset.

♪♪♪

Henry has three enormously dominant Side B Behaviors he has chosen to walk in each day to make a difference, influence others, and achieve results. With the power of a Leadership Playlist, he is also choosing the music that feeds his behaviors.

What are those behaviors?

First, you might be able to see that Henry is the **Drummer**: powerful and skilled with asking the right questions to lead the company forward. Most talented CEOs are curious. He starts by setting up small, cross-functional team lunches just to talk and ask them questions about what they encounter each day.

Secondly, Henry is the **Pianist**: skilled at mentoring people with discipline and sincerity. Henry makes it noticeably clear to his leadership team that getting to know your people does not mean an acceptance of a loss of results. Instead, he finds that when people enjoy what they do, they will be disciplined to get the job done and feel valued for the work they do.

Finally, Henry is the **Saxophonist**: he believes in a culture of listening—a place where people are heard, seen, and valued. He is at last able to see that his forgotten or put-on-the-back-burner "people skills" led to a culture of skepticism, mistrust, and disrespect. He is now ready to listen.

♪♪♪

As leaders, we are results-driven and know how to execute on our Side A skills, behaviors, and competencies. After all, they are what put us in our role. However, by tapping into music, we get the chance to develop our Side B behavioral skills to bring the next level of leadership—and our whole self—to serve those who need us. We are the teachers, coaches, mentors, and inspiration for those climbing the ladders today, and it is our responsibility to show them what it means to look at business through the lens of our whole self, as a person *and* a leader.

When you combine your Side A and Side B, the ideas flow, growth is inevitable, and productivity is rewarding because people are craving your participation and enjoying the collaboration and their time in the work environment. We are at a pivotal crossroads. Our people need us; they are highly fatigued, facing uncertainty and feeling disconnected. What I want you to take away from this message is that the most captivating leaders make us feel like we're listening to a great song! We are inspired, fueled, and ready to begin anything.

Are you ready to bring your whole self to your leadership and lead from both Side A and Side B skills, competencies, and behaviors? It takes courage and strength, but I know you have it in you.

Without further ado, let's get back to the band.

THE VIOLINIST: CERTAIN

I would now like to introduce you to the **Violinist** or the **Certain Legacy Behavior**. If you lead with the Certain Legacy Behavior, you walk with an aura of confidence and swag surrounding you, yet it is unpretentious. As the violinist, you must be precise and certain to the placement of where the bow will land (or your business plans). With four strings and a bow, you are rich in tone and dynamics and not afraid to experiment.

There is something very special about this Legacy Behavior. It is understood that while violinists are confident risk-takers, they are also very conscientious about doing what is right and have a natural ability to influence others with certainty and joy.

If your Legacy is Certain, we are hungry for your advice, knowledge, and confidence.

♪♪♪

"Trying to please everybody is impossible—if you did that,
you'd end up in the middle with nobody liking you.
You've just got to make the decision about
what you think is your best and do it."
—*John Lennon*

Laurel Scheaf is the first President and CEO of est (Erhard Seminars Training) and on the board of directors and accountable for the development of forum leaders at Landmark Worldwide (a personal growth, training, and development company). I defined the behavior in the Certain Legacy after her specifically. I had always looked up to her; however, when my father passed, I looked to her even more to fill the business gap in my heart that once was my father.

As a reminder, the Certain Legacy has conviction and confidence, with realist optimism. This leader is not afraid to try new things and looks towards the future for ideas. Yes, this describes my Aunt Laurel.

As a strong woman leader, I wanted to understand the path she chose and the decisions she made in her career. What I learned is that she has an adventurous side and certainty with her decisions, and her goal in life is to make a difference. When she was 16, after hearing "I Left My Heart in San Francisco" by Tony Bennett, she immediately thought, *If I am not married by the end of college, I am going to San Francisco.*

When that day finally rolled around, she was graduating with a degree in high school history and math. But on the day before graduation, she had a nightmare that startled her because she was about to teach school and had no idea how to truly make a difference. She realized that only 3 teachers in her 16 years of school had really made a difference with *her* learning, and she didn't know what to do to make that real difference with her students at the time. So, she decided in the next moment, like a flash, that she was not going to teach. She was also supposed to get engaged the summer of her college graduating year; however, he got scared and backed out. She only cried for about three minutes—truthfully!

Therefore, she called one of her sorority sisters and asked if she would like to move to San Francisco with her and get a job there. They had never been west of the Mississippi, but off they went to San Francisco, just as she said she would. Upon arrival in San Francisco, she started to look at the ads in the *San Francisco Chronicle* to find a job. She stumbled across a great ad that read, "Women Only: How would you like to drink champagne, eat hot dogs, and jet-set around the world?" She had just turned 21, was single, and thought it would be perfect.

Being her niece, I had to ask her if she was concerned or afraid. Her answer?

"No, not a bit. I'm not really afraid of much of anything." As an adventurous soul, it did not occur to her to be afraid.

The job was simple enough. She was to show a set of books to mothers with small children. Understand, there were not many preschools at the time (in 1967), and these books were founded on the development of Dr. Glen Dolman. Dolman showed that children from 1 to 6 years of age learn the fastest, and if mothers would spend just 10 minutes a day with these books, the children would be prepared for school. So, Laurel knocked on a door, handed them a letter, introduced herself, and asked if she could come in and present the book set. Most mothers let her into their homes, and as she gave her 20-minute presentation, she heard questions being answered that they, as book saleswomen, were not asking. The biggest question not being asked was the simplest: "As a mother, what do you need to do to make a difference with your children, so they are prepared for school?"

Laurel saw that in real life, these mothers simply wanted to make a difference, and she had the courage to start speaking to what mattered to people.

However, for two weeks, she had not written any contracts and needed to pay rent. She walked into her boss Werner's office and said, "I am either going to write three sales today, or I am going to quit." Of course, she didn't want to quit, which is precisely why she put that reality at stake. She was out in the field until 9:30 p.m. that day, and she finished writing those three sales. She says, "That is when I discovered that my word was much bigger than the thoughts, doubts, questions, and all the noise that flies around in my head."

In 1971, Werner Erhard started the company est (Erhard Seminars Training), and he asked Laurel to be the president and CEO to bring the company and product (the est training) into existence. She began by generating attendees for the seminars. They started with a 100-person event, and Laurel remembered that her word meant something. The first training itself only had 32 people in it. But the profound difference that the event made with each person was something she had never seen before. Seeing that difference, she gave her word to have a 250-person event and started communicating, inviting, sharing, and standing for what would continue to make a difference for people.

She believes the biggest takeaway here is that when you stop thinking about how you are going to keep your word and just keep it, things happen. You must fight for your word over your doubts, fears, and questioning. If you do not, nobody else will. Ultimately, her word was connected to making a real, lasting difference. Laurel tells me that her motto is "Live not to regret anything."

In 2020, Aunt Laurel retired after answering that one ad. She is certain that she made a difference, and living up to her word and working for one company for an entire career is incredible. Even when she went through the ups and downs of life, keeping her word to make a difference grounded her certainty.

How can you spot the **Violinist** behaving in their **Certain Legacy**?

1. "Decisive decisions with certainty" is their motto.

2. They are confident and walk with swag.

3. They enjoy generating new ideas and taking risks.

4. They show complete conviction about what they believe in.

5. They influence others naturally.

THE CONGA DRUMS: COURAGEOUS

I would next like to introduce you to the **Conga Drums**, or the **Courageous Legacy Behavior**. If you lead with courage, you

 stand in strength and do not fear change. You are easily adaptable. Have you heard the conga drums? They are so simple yet produce such bold sounds. You probably have a crisis management plan prepared, and if not, you are ready and willing to face any obstacle head-on with courage and readiness.

This is what leading with a Courageous Legacy looks like— seeing people through tough situations with support and execution. You will not be deterred or defensive.

♪♪♪

"Without deviation from the norm, progress is not possible."
—*Frank Zappa*

Rakhi Voria, Director of Global Digital Sales Development for IBM, has led her life not only being courageous but walking in the courageous *legacy*. She is a child of Indian immigrants, raised in Colorado by a single mom for whom she feels grateful for showing her what success, discipline, and courage look like. Her mother was always an agent of change in the community, never letting hardships set her back. Today, her mother is a CEO, an internationally recognized speaker, a U.S.-India expert, and even served as an advisor to the Obama Administration on minority business enterprises.

Rakhi said that the lessons her mom taught her and the values she instilled in her growing up have undoubtedly shaped her into the courageous leader and businesswoman she is today.

She has always been interested in experimenting with new things and ideas, yet has had the courage to switch to a better plan or strategy when necessary. Rakhi feels that studying at Oxford opened the door to see and challenge herself in the next step in life: working in technology. Through her studies, she realized that the world was becoming borderless and that business was globalizing. She saw the challenges that people faced all over the world surrounding access to education, healthcare, welfare, and economic security and realized that she wanted to work for a company that had the ability to do something about it.

Being flexible and adaptable to change is a strength of Rakhi's, and her upbringing greatly contributed to and helped develop her courage and confidence. She says, "I was interested in working in an industry that was committed to making a difference and ended up joining Microsoft after attending a recruiting event at Oxford. I was attracted to Microsoft's mission to empower every person and every organization on the planet to achieve more, and I had seen the impact that technology had made even in my own life growing up. The beauty of working at multinational corporations is that you can take on horizontal challenges while still growing vertically. There's a growth mindset and a culture of learning in the technology field where people are encouraged to try roles across a variety of divisions, and I'm grateful to have had varying experiences across different business functions and companies."

Rakhi courageously steps into opportunities to strategize and make things better. For example, advancing women in business and technology is important to her. Her upbringing sparked Rakhi's commitment to breaking down barriers for women and building a more inclusive society. Therefore, she currently serves as the Executive Co-Chair of the Women@IBM group in NYC, which is designed to help IBM women grow their professional skills and expand career options through access to resources and tools. Rakhi says that leading this group has allowed her to exercise her passion for supporting, advancing, and retaining female talent in the workplace while also building partnerships with similar groups at other companies.

Rakhi certainly has the courage to try new approaches and change course when needed.

How can you spot the **Conga Drums** behaving in their **Courageous Legacy**?

1. "Implementation with courage" is their motto.

2. They are open to flexibility and open to change.

3. They are exceptional at heading off problems.

4. People admire their versatility and bravery.

5. They tend to sit in the background until they are needed.

THE SAXOPHONE: GRACIOUS

Next, I would like to introduce you to **the Saxophonist**, or the **Gracious Legacy Behavior**. If you lead with this legacy, you are rich in self-awareness, and your depth of gratitude shows no bounds. You are diverse in thought, listen with intentionality, and provide a safe space to share and reflect. Just like the saxophone, your uniqueness is contagious. Your team will go that extra mile for you because they feel appreciated.

If your legacy is graciousness, you are respected for your uniqueness. Not many leaders have the ability to achieve results with love, but you do. You come from a place of gratitude, and because of that, you are more likely to overachieve on your goals.

♪♪♪

"Music touches us emotionally, where words alone can't."
—*Johnny Depp*

John Barrows, CEO of JB Sales Training, James Buckley, and I sat down for a conversation about the leaders of the future. This was arranged by James, who works with John, and explained to me that John is the best leader he has ever had—and that is something all leaders should strive to be! I had been following John Barrows for a while, but I wanted to see what James was talking about.

They each took the survey and uncovered that they both share the Gracious Legacy Behavior.

I wanted to understand John's mindset on leadership, and he was humbled by the opportunity and very forthcoming. He believes that no matter how successful you are or what success looks like to you, what matters most are the core values you live with, your level of engagement with your teams, and your understanding that positive behavior goes a long way. He believes that while he is the owner of the business, everyone contributes and has an opinion, and he is thankful that they are on this journey with him.

While there are times John battles pessimism, it is gratitude that pulls him into the future. He and his 10-year-old daughter have created an acronym they use to help them stay focused on what they can control: EAT! Effort, Attitude, and how we Treat People. John says, "We can't control a lot of things in life, but we *can* control our effort and how hard we work, our attitude, how positive or negative it is, and how we treat people with kindness, respect, and dignity." I can only imagine that this is why James feels so inspired and empowered to do his work!

Throughout our conversation, John spoke from a very real space of gratitude, and I know he leads with a systematic yet gracious approach.

James and John both talk about what they call the "future leader." This leader must show up authentically and be open to conversations while committing to truly listen. They must be both diplomatic and empathetic, ready to show grace and return kindness, and yet be real with people about the job they are doing. This means that if you are not doing the job they hired you to do, there are consequences! And those conversations can be hurtful; however, they are meant to help you grow both personally and professionally. That is our job as leaders.

When I asked James what it was like to work with John, he went on to describe a partnership I believe he called a "Flatline Organizational Chart," where there is a healthy hierarchy of authority, and no one feels "below the line" without a voice. While it is John's company, and he is ultimately responsible for the organization, he wants us, those who work at his company, to be a part of the journey.

I want to share this comment in James's own words: "John is the only person I have ever worked for that runs a truly flat organization in every instance—our opinions, our aspirations, our goals, and our submissions to the team. When we want to talk about our goals, dreams, and opinions, he gives us his time. I can't tell you how many leaders I've worked for that don't have time for me."

Unfortunately, I hear this a lot, and to walk in gratitude, leaders must be humble, open to listening, helpful, and results-oriented. It is within a culture of gratitude that your workforce will come to you and openly share their thoughts and opinions. All you need to do is listen.

How can you spot the **Saxophonist** behaving in their **Gracious Legacy**?

1. "Determination with grace" is their motto.
2. They are extremely smart yet humbled to serve others and show appreciation.
3. They radiate warmth and empathy for others; however, they are diplomatic with business.
4. They seek understanding with kindness and actions.
5. "Flip the Organizational Chart" is not just words to them—they live it out daily.

THE HARMONICA: KIND

Last but not least, I would like to introduce the final instrument and Legacy Behavior: the **Harmonica**, or the **Kindness Legacy Behavior**. If you lead with this legacy, you are very powerful in your ability to achieve and make goals, and you speak from both your heart and mind—just like the harmonica sound can be both soft and pointed at the same time. It's in your nature to stay positive and remember that everyone has something happening in their life, and your goal is to be supportive through it all. Although this does not distract you from making tough decisions or taking disciplinary action, you have a softer edge when necessary. People appreciate that authenticity.

If your legacy is kindness, you are a very special leader. You go out of your way, sometimes to a fault, to provide encouragement and help your teams or anyone that needs help.

♪♪♪

"For me there is something primitively soothing about this music, and it went straight to my nervous system, making me feel 10 feet tall."
—*Eric Clapton*

In the broad sense of a corporate environment, is being kind considered "sucking up" or being weak? Think about this for a moment. Oftentimes, being open-minded and helpful seems to be questioned. I find this to be very upsetting because it is in kindness that the world changes with collaboration and creativity. Are employees unconditionally kind to their leaders, or do they say a different thing behind their backs? Maybe there is a reason for their supposed kindness, like hopes of a promotion or more responsibility. And when *leaders* show kindness to their teams, is it only at a departmental level? What about all levels of leadership? Does kindness only travel upstream because there is not enough time to travel downstream? Listen, I have heard all these questions from people before, and yes, this conversation goes through a lot of our minds.

The Kindness Legacy is *authentically* helpful, friendly, and considerate of people. Authenticity is the sign of a great leader. If inauthentic, many people fall short of greatness. Now, let me be clear: Being a responsible employee, worker, teammate, and leader in business is to produce revenue and growth for the company. Results, productivity, and data are necessary to build a profitable company. Thus, it is in words and action that kindness is contagious.

I once had a leader that would leave a simple letter of appreciation on my work anniversary. It was personal, spoke to something I learned in the past year, and encouraged my growth with a tip. A small and simple act of kindness like this can pay great dividends with retention, tenacity, and going that extra mile the company may need sometimes. The more helpful, friendly, and collaborative a culture that a company can instill, the more that results will follow.

Tom Dekle, a Client Executive for IBM I admire very much, is certainly knowledgeable in the kindness arena and shows up in this behavior consistently. Tom knows that each person is a gift and might be fighting some monster in their life—anxiety, heartache, people, society, to name a few—and they need the strength to stand up and say, "No way, not today, you will not get me down!" A kind leader sees this and can help someone stand up.

Kindness is also contagious. People spend most of their waking hours at work, and being appreciated makes a difference in every area of their lives.

One of the most important things a leader can do to support their team is to know what they want from their career and offer to help. For example, Tom believes that people have a specific image of themselves in a career and know what they can or cannot do. Sometimes they might be looking at their own career or job and say to themselves, "I am struggling; how can I enjoy this role or process if I'm like *that*?"—whatever "that" may mean in their eyes. However, it is our job as leaders to recognize their struggle and help them look at the totality of what they are accomplishing with what they *are* doing. Helping them see a different perspective can change their mindset and get them out of the negativity they are feeling. Reminding them of the people they meet and influence, for instance, allows our people to continue to work, build and understand that their job is a part of the *whole* self. We will all have good, bad, and even ugly days, but we all need reminders, every so often, that humanity is at the core of kindness.

A kind leader also seeks to understand if their team is happy and always open to a conversation. Kindness for people outweighs the drama that not being kind will create; therefore, take care of your people, and they will do amazing things and drive incredible results. The rest will take care of itself.

How can you spot the **Harmonica** behaving in their **Kindness Legacy**?

1. "Accountability with kindness" is their motto.
2. They genuinely care for their team's growth and professional development.
3. Their support is generous and unconditional.
4. When discipline is necessary, they are transparent and speak from understanding.
5. They are altruists by nature, ensuring fairness for all.

WHAT MUSICIAN SPEAKS TO YOU?

From my perspective, that is both an easy and difficult question to answer. What I *can* tell you is that in my life, I needed clarity to bring my whole self. Once I decluttered and unplugged from all the other "noise," I could finally see my own Side B Band, my whole self, and what was missing or needed developing. Yes, my band sounds a little out of tune, as I am still practicing those instruments that I want to develop a greater strength in.

We all have stories, struggles, weights, and scars; I am no different. However, as I began to listen to more music, I started to recognize that my mindset was shifting. I didn't like to be told what I am, how to believe, or what to do. I needed to complete that part of me to clean up the ugly and bring my whole self back to people.

If you are a leader, I implore you to take the time to understand your team's individual goals, passions, strengths, and weaknesses and work with them, giving them an opportunity to grow. It's important not to punish them with the rhetoric of corporate talk, ignoring their goals and dreams, or to simply dismiss them by going around them to achieve your own success. Remember Pat from Henry's story? If you have a team or individual that can execute, provide good results, and is a cultural fit, show up for them! Don't be the leader who fails their people!

Keeping all Side B Band Legacies in mind, I ask: Do you want to excel at just one behavior, or do you want to be a multiplatinum record with a complete band? Personally, I want the whole band, not only within myself but for those who surround me. When I was leading teams and hiring managers, I learned that the best way for me to approach the interviewing process was to look for people who could complement my band, who were better at a few instruments than I was, and who were not afraid to respectfully speak their opinions. I had the opportunity to build a management team by taking this musical mindset to hire right, and that, my friend, I couldn't have learned by watching, waiting, emulating, and filtering my strengths.

As you've learned through these pages, I chose music! Mostly because there is no judgment in music, and I have no time for self-judgment. Furthermore, it was through music

I finally felt complete. I can bring kindness and creativity, discipline and grace into my leadership song, and I am ready to share it with my family, friends, and coworkers, who are extraordinary people and a joy to be around.

As I mentioned earlier, this is your journey, your song to complete, and it will be as unique as you are. However, regardless of the journey you take and the Legacy Behavior you embody, the people you serve will feel empowered, engaged, loyal, and work hard for you—the extraordinary leader.

It's time to be you!

Song: "It's Time To Be You"
It's not about the titles or gettin' the fame
It's about that work you stamp with your name
It's not about the goals you set or achieve, it's time to dream big
It's time to be you

Lyrics by Paula White

CHAPTER 7

MAKE YOUR LEADERSHIP PLAYLIST

"No matter what happens in life, be good to people.
Being good to people is a wonderful legacy to leave behind."
—*Taylor Swift*

Henry has just returned from a week-long vacation in St. John
U.S.V.I. with his family. His wife, Sue, and the kids were
ecstatic to see their father relaxed and ready to play for the first
time. Henry even chose to sign an agreement with his four executive members and kept his word to only look at his work for
a half-hour in the morning, before the family got up, and a
half-hour in the evening before dinner. He is rested, relaxed,
and re-energized, with even more ideas to create more business.

On his way into work Monday morning, Henry is listening
to the 15-minute playlist he created for the drive to get his
mind mentally prepared for the day. The first song he hears is
one that his kids recommended for him, "Treat People with

Kindness" by Harry Styles. When he arrives, his first stop is Pat's office. He sits down and asks Pat a question: "How are you doing, my friend?"

For the first time in a long time, Henry feels complete. He can take time for both the organization and his family. However, he had to do the work, learn not to fear the emotions of people, and uncover his song. He has three very strong emotional behaviors to lead with that he can use to serve his people, and his band is growing.

ARE YOU READY TO HIT "PLAY"?

Every person on earth has a specific musical preference. It could be pop, jazz, country, classical, hip-hop, grunge, or punk, to name a few. Just like your Legacy Behavior, personality, strengths, and weaknesses are unique to you, so are your preferences and playlists. This is important to remember because music choices are very personal. Whatever your unique preferences are, you can categorize them into a playlist to fit your mood or the motivation you need.

While Spotify might be able to create a playlist to boost your mood or chill you out, it is up to *you* to curate a work playlist. This is a group of songs you can listen to while driving to work, during a break, or even late at night in the office—which I know you all have on occasion!

There are many places to start. The first step is to become aware of your natural Legacy Behavior and be ready to fully share it with the people you serve.

We always have the choice between intention or action, and as I finished writing this book, I found that the power of music drove my intention into action. Music will give you the sound and beats to bring your positive Legacy Behavior to the surface. Some might say that it is impossible to have such a monumental shift by simply listening to music, but I assure you it is not. Taking a chance to develop your leadership never comes without challenges or the disruption of the everyday business grind, but with intentional action, your music will help you throughout the day, and people will begin to see the authentic you!

Trust me; we will continue to have days of distraction and make mistakes; however, extraordinary leaders who choose to walk in *their* legacy will benefit their organization and the people they serve. Therefore, it is important to show up in your legacy and truly get to know and understand the people you work with every day.

Do you recall when you first started your career? I bet you were on the edge of your seat looking for positive recognition or, like me, wanted to keep your head down and hoped that others would see you for all your hard work. Either way, people naturally have a desire to learn, build a career, and grow within a company. But let's face it, today we are living in an age of disruption, and people are craving leadership that requires A.L.L. of you. Disruption? Yes, jobs may be plentiful, yet retention numbers are down, and technology has given rise to more efficiency and a do-it-quicker attitude that disrupts our ability to be ourselves while building a career. The time is now to hit "play" and lead authentically.

HAS YOUR MUSIC STOPPED?

Before we know it, music as a milestone marker trails off, as we discussed. We get busy, and our focused time takes over, creativity gives way to problem-solving, and we begin to live a life of triage. Yet we get the promotions, recognition, and salary hikes. Leading becomes doing, accomplishing, and achieving great results. Therefore, let's take a nostalgic trip back to before the silence and work to uncover the music deep within:

1. What was your favorite song when you were?

   a. 8-10 years old: _____

   b. 15-20 years old: _____

   c. 25-35 years old: _____

   d. Today: _____

2. What was the first concert you attended? _____

   a. Why? _____

   b. With whom did you go? _____

   c. What year was it and what was your age? _____

3. What was the last concert you attended? _____

Are you able to recognize a pattern? Are they joyous songs, rebellious songs, or have your creative music tastes changed? Now is the time to take an opportunity to review your memories and determine if the music has been turned off in your life to make way for the busy corporate grind. Do you still mark your successes, events, and achievements with music, or have you been sitting in silence? It is in the silence, as we work on our laptops, write emails, create presentations, and analyze data, that we can lose touch with who we really are. Here is the beautiful thing: Now that you've looked back, you are able to look forward and begin to create *your* Legacy Playlist.

CREATING YOUR LEGACY PLAYLIST

As mentioned earlier, when you attach memories, motivations, and actions to music, your leadership song begins to form. You are now just a few steps away from bringing your whole self and your A.L.L. into your career and living a life you love and enjoy. This probably will be the first time you have considered a playlist for work to motivate you and bring clarity and focus. Think of the lyrics as sending a message to you. For example, "Haven't Met You Yet" by Michael Bublé could be a song about not meeting yourself yet, or "Secrets" by OneRepublic could speak to you as a leader about the need to be collaborative. It's up to you to choose the song and apply the meaning you hear. As you create your playlist, let it be unique to you as a leader. Here is a way to begin.

1. **Write** down a few of your favorite songs. If you're stuck, here are a few ways you can search for music:

   • Dig through your old albums.

   • Listen to your preferred channels and let your mind start working. I used to listen to the '60s, '70s, and '80s curated lists developed for listeners on Spotify. When a song would play that I remembered and liked, I took a snapshot of it on my cell phone to remember. I started listening to a lot of extraordinarily good music again.

- Google your favorite artists.
- Do a YouTube search for your favorite artists, and then get sucked down the rabbit hole of music with the recommended videos that follow.
- Don't stay in one decade or one genre! Mix it up.
- Explore new music.

2. **Listen** to the full song and ask yourself the following questions:

- What does it do to my soul, my heart, and my mind?
- Do the words resonate with my Legacy Behavior?
- Does the beat motivate me and get me moving?
  - If so, write it down and put two thoughts as to why it moves you towards that behavior.
  - If you are having trouble, Google words that relate to your Legacy Behavior. For example, I Googled "kindness songs" and found articles that listed off hundreds of songs. However, again, you must relate to the song and put your legacy meaning behind it.

3. **Create** your own unique playlist of 10-30 songs.

- Begin to listen to your playlist each morning before work, after work, and at any time you feel you are drifting from your Legacy Behavior. You may not have to listen to the full playlist; maybe just one or two songs will be able to shape your mindset.

4. **Execute**: Playing music at the *right* time is an enormously powerful tool to have in your toolbox. Remember, you "get to" apply what it means to you and how it can help you walk in your Side B Behavior Legacy. Will you motivate, inspire, or teach today?

    • Start thinking of ways you can motivate, innovate, and share what a song means. For example, your team just had a record month, and you are exhausted from the grind. What can you do? Well, it depends. Do you already have a theme for the year to achieve results? If so, walk in the office either playing that song on a speaker or send your team a link to YouTube in the morning so when they arrive, they are greeted with the song. If you don't have a theme for the year, maybe "Celebration" by Kool & the Gang would be appropriate—or maybe not. If it were me, I would start the day with "Kung Fu Fighting" by Carl Douglas!

The power of music in businesses like retail, entertainment, and restaurants is incredible; they already know the importance of setting the mood for an experience. If we took their logic and applied it to our corporate offices, we might just see people enjoying their careers and getting creative while we watch retention rise. Just some food... no, *music* for thought!

THAT ONE SONG

Sometimes you won't have time for a full playlist, so prepare yourself now. Find one song that will fight for your moods, clarity, peace, and space. You most likely will have different songs for different needs, but whichever ones you pick, have them ready so you can hit "play" right away and not waste time searching for one in the moment. Your songs will likely change over time, and that is okay (and sometimes necessary).

Here are a few examples of scenarios you can start finding songs for:

- To start your morning
- To keep you focused, not frustrated
- To lift you up when you are down
- To help you when you are overwhelmed
- To create space for clarity
- To bring you strength and encouragement
- To declutter your mind
- To slow down the negative self-talk
- To keep your ego in check
- To motivate yourself or your team

MUSICAL PREFERENCE

Another great tool is to take the Musical Universe assessment. Included in Dr. Greenberg's assessment, which you can take by visiting https://musicaluniverse.io/. On this site you will find the most recent advance in music preference research and how it has shown that we can organize our musical preferences into five distinct dimensions: Mellow, Unpretentious, Sophisticated, Intense, and Contemporary music (conveniently named the MUSIC Preference Model).[1]

CONNECT YOUR REMARKABLE SIDE B TO MUSIC

As you get ready to go on this journey of living your Authentic Leadership Legacy, remember, it is not only using music as a resource but as a metaphor for your positive behaviors. Once those behaviors are awakened, you will feel the pull at your heartstrings and be able to use that emotion logically in business. To create a unique Leadership Playlist, you must first hear your song play in your heart and trust how those emotions are leading you on a path to connect it all together.

As you journey on your path, you may find you need a little help starting your unique Leadership Playlist. I started one for you on Spotify that you can reference if you find yourself in need of encouragement or empowerment to get started. Just hover over the QR Code with the camera on your phone! These lists are broken down by Legacy Behavior below:

[1] Rentfrow, P. J., Goldberg, L. R. & Levitin, D. J. The structure of musical preferences: A five-factor model. J. Pers. Soc. Psychol. (2011). doi:10.1037/a0022406

The Drummer: Curious

Self-improvement is a lifelong process, not a stage of life like going to college. You have an opportunity to learn from any situation or any person you encounter. This is precisely like the Drummer's Behavior envisioning the future by being open and experimenting. Asking questions is your trademark for progression and self-improvement. If you lead with the Curious Legacy Behavior, here are some tips and tricks for you to grow:

- Ask for feedback often from those around you that you trust. "What do you think of how I led that meeting?" or "What do you think I could have done better today?" are examples of common questions you can ask.

- Make a list of all the ways you could improve yourself. Then prioritize and make specific plans and commit to an improvement plan for yourself; find an accountability buddy.

- Playlist starts: "I Gotta Feeling" by Black Eyed Peas or "Question" by The Moody Blues. *Tip: This is a great song for Inside Salespeople!*

Spotify Playlist: The Drummer – Curious

The Lead Guitarist: Passionate

Having enthusiasm for your goals is motivating because it connects you to your work objectives. However, sometimes your enthusiasm can be low because your goals are not clear, or you need a change so that you CAN get excited about your job and your objectives. If your goals are unclear or not aligned properly, you might consider these things:

- Take time to reflect on your career goals. What is most motivating to you vs. least motivating to you?

- What aspects of your job can perhaps be adjusted, delegated, or reviewed so you are more connected to goals that are truly exciting and motivating for you?

- What might be some quick wins in terms of results you can achieve to give you greater connection with your goals? Then, you can build on these to generate greater excitement and enthusiasm.

- Playlist starts: "Fight Song" by Rachel Platten or "I'm Gonna Be (500 Miles)" by the Proclaimers. *Tip: Think that you're going to be the leader your team needs.*

Spotify Playlist: The Lead Guitarist – Passionate

The Bass Guitarist: Ethical

As the Bass Guitarist, you naturally influence others just by listening. Knowing that listening is fundamental to serving people, you take extra steps to be intentional with all your conversations, raising them to a higher level in the space of integrity, allowing for people to be heard. Here are some tips and tricks for you to grow in your Legacy Behavior:

- Think of the many ways what you do helps others.

- What positive impact do you have on the world around you?

- What are some additional ways you might find to help others to increase your positive impact?

- What causes do you feel strongly about that you might get involved with to give you greater fulfillment and satisfaction?

- If you were to stop doing something that is borderline unethical or honest, what would it be? Make a plan to turn that situation around so that you feel even better about your impact and connection with others.

- Playlist starts: "Man in The Mirror" by Michael Jackson or "Integrity Blues" by Jimmy Eat World.

Spotify Playlist: The Bass Guitarist – Ethical

The Pianist: Sincere

The Pianist is not afraid to make decisions and will accept responsibility for them. If you lead with the Sincere Legacy Behavior, you are intentional about your decisions and consider both the risks and the rewards. Some leaders may take the easy route and pass off decisions to others so that they don't risk getting blamed or making a mistake. But this is not how you roll. Instead, you are confident in your approach. Think of decision-making as a growth exercise. Here are a few ways you can approach this growth:

- Think deeply about the decisions you are hesitant to make. What is getting in your way? How can you face those fears and start small by making some low-risk attempts to be more decisive?

- List some decisions you need to make in the future. What are the consequences if you do NOT make the decision? What are the consequences if you DO make the decision?

- If you are prone to worry and rumination, practice making a decision and then letting go emotionally. Stop yourself when your self-talk becomes obsessive or critical.

- Playlist starts: "I'll Stand by You" by the Pretenders, "Morning of Our Lives" by Jonathan Richman and the Modern Lovers, or "I Got a Name" by Jim Croce. *Tip: Being sincere is remembering everyone on your team has a name and is valued.*

Spotify Playlist: The Pianist – Sincere

The Rhythm Guitarist: Trustworthy

The Rhythm Guitarist not only wants to be challenged and enjoys the process of planning, but also finds success in their preference for collaboration. If you lead from this Legacy Behavior, you are fully aware that collaboration improves the quality of decision-making and makes implementation smoother because involving people in the process builds trust and increases engagement. Inviting input from others is not a sign of weakness or lack of confidence. In fact, it builds your reputation as a collaborative force for good. Here are some ideas to help you collaborate more:

- Involving others in the decision-making process is likely to increase their understanding rather than them blindly following orders. Make sure they understand the "why" behind requested actions.

- Collaboration does not mean that you give up power. It does not mean taking a poll and going with the majority. It means that you collect valuable input and use that collective intelligence to make a better and more informed decision.

- Remember: Asking for input does not commit you to following what you hear. Agreement is not required, but posing intelligent questions is.

- Playlist starts: "Trust in Me" by Etta James or "Trust In You" by Lauren Daigle.

Spotify Playlist: The Rhythm Guitarist – Trustworthy

The Vocalist: Optimistic

An Optimistic leader perceives people's strengths and helps them build on these while simultaneously inspiring them to improve upon their weaknesses. In this way, employees are inspired to give their individual best. Optimism also has the power to propel people to act. If your personal level of optimism is not high, you may need to make some changes in your own life. Here are three ways you can use this superpower to cultivate influence:

- Look introspectively at your organization and your own behavior to create a vision for your teams to see a path that is worth trusting.

- As their leader, share your optimism with the people you serve. Be sure to call out their strengths and bring them up higher.

- Build enthusiasm and create a culture of success. This is the greatest benefit your optimistic attitude will bring!

- Playlist starts: "Mr. Blue Sky" by Electric Light Orchestra or "Upside Down" by Set It Off. *Tip: Keeping your optimism realistic is a superpower!*

Spotify Playlist: The Vocalist – Optimistic

The Violinist: Certain

We understand that certainty is having complete conviction about a topic, idea, or vision. It is the passion of the Violinist to experiment with realistic optimism. Experimenting is, simply put, trying out new concepts or ways of doing things. This can mean trying out a business strategy on a small scale. An example might be test marketing a new product to a narrow audience of consumers, such as those in one city. Technology companies are constantly experimenting, as it is the engine that drives innovation. If you want to experiment more, here are some ideas:

- Experimenting can be simply running an investigation or test of a current process or method. What is working well, what could be improved, and what could be tweaked to make it slightly better?

- Read the *Havard Business Review* article from 2011: "A Step-by-Step Guide to Smart Business Experiments."

- Playlist starts: "High Hopes" by Panic! at The Disco or "Best Day of My Life" by American Authors.

Spotify Playlist: The Violinist – Certain

The Conga Drummer: Courage

"The only constant in life is change," said an ancient Greek philosopher by the name of Heraclitus more than 2,000 years ago. Absolutely nothing is permanent, stable, predictable, or constant throughout the universe—except change itself. Many of us are uncomfortable with the fact that change is completely uncontrollable. However, the Conga Drummer is courageous about change, facing it head-on, even the discomfort of it. They are naturally able to flex and adapt easily to change because it is with their gift of courage that they find their strength. Change also brings opportunity, of course. Even a change that seems like misfortune can be turned into good fortune. If you lead with this Legacy Behavior, here are a few thoughts to consider:

- What changes have impacted you over your career, both positive and negative ones?

- What changes are you experiencing right now?

- What changes have you experienced that seemed negative but had a silver lining somehow?

- Playlist starts: "Courage" by Pink or "Three Little Birds" by Bob Marley.

Spotify Playlist: The Conga Drummer – Courage

The Saxophonist: Gracious

Part of being gracious is communicating with tact and diplomacy. Take a minute to read your audience, and instead of blurting out what you need or want, ask the other person how they are feeling, what is new in their world, or comment on something you know about them to get them talking with you before you get to the point. Put yourself in the other person's shoes before you start talking. This builds trust and rapport. Here are a few ways to build upon this Legacy Behavior:

- Focus on what you want the person to do rather than what they are doing wrong.

- Ask people if there is anything you said to them that could have been put more diplomatically. Thank them for the feedback, and apologize for any insensitivity you displayed.

- Playlist starts: "Lean on Me" by Bill Withers or "Bright Side of the Road" by Van Morrison.

Spotify Playlist: The Saxophonist – Gracious

The Harmonica: Kind

When we think of kindness, generally, people expect to see behaviors such as friendliness, consideration, and generosity. Like harmonicas accompanying a song, mentors and coaches who show an interest in serving people strongly demonstrate this behavior. Mentors/coaches are open and reflective and usually invite input from others. They don't have to have all the answers themselves, yet they always strive to be helpful. They are resourceful, not always the ultimate expert. Be the kind of coach who has a variety of skilled contacts. You may not have all the answers yourself, but you can find the answer through your network. Constantly build your network through your generosity and collaboration. Watch for when people need your help and support, then offer it. Here are a few ideas to get you going:

- Be kind but also be candid and honest.

- When you offer feedback, make sure it is done in a kind, constructive way.

- Playlist starts: "Keep Your Head Up" by Andy Grammer or "Treat People with Kindness" by Harry Styles.

Spotify Playlist: The Harmonica – Kind

IT'S TIME TO BE YOU!

How far can you go with your Leadership Playlist? As far as you want!

Is your personal song finished or your playlist full? If not, it is now up to you.

Your playlist choices help you to engage with the real you, be an inspiration to future leaders, and create a positive culture and a kind community.

What about creating a playlist to transition from work to home life to be present with your family, friends, and loved ones? Create a vision for a vacation and develop a family playlist to listen to together leading up to departure.

What five minutes can you spare to have a song ready to go that will create space for conversation with family members or other things that are on the back burner?

Music is now a gift that you have in your toolbox to explore creativity, stay focused, have clarity of words or ideas, rest, and become the type of leader beyond what you envision.

It's time to be you! Leadership is about change. It's about creating an inner playlist that will inspire you to lead with your heart, produce results, and help others. I heard a brilliant speaker talking about how taking the time to wander—whether in nature, around the block, or in your mind—is necessary for the growth of the culture, environment, company, and yourself. I will take it a step further here. If you take the time to wander through your music choices and listen to the expression of rhythm and melody, you are well on your way.

What if you began to think of leadership in terms of having all the skills, both résumé and emotion-based ones, to serve people and show up in your Authentic Leadership Legacy—your whole self? Music will guide you on a path of creativity, focus, and clarity. As hard-working leaders who have focused on building your business and achieving results, please choose not to lose sight of your gift to truly serve people. With a musical mindset you can learn to remix your leadership style and open your heart to your "people" gift—your Side B Legacy Behaviors. They are the best part of you. **Don't keep them silent!**

This is your journey, and you have the power to choose your lyrics, your tempo, your rhythm—your song. It's time for others to hear your **Side B** song loud and clear. You will see that walking in your Authentic Leadership Legacy will have a compound effect on you, your results, and the people you lead.

What if you could recognize that your Side B Behavior is as equally important as your Side A résumé achievements?

What if you understood how music affects your mindset and ultimately impacts your leadership language?

What if transformation, taking a risk, and being courageous and confident could impact your life and career?

What if you were willing to experiment with new ideas and be willing to take a chance and have faith in the results and growth?

What if you could hear the music playing again?

Music is the path to Side B, Side B is the path to authenticity, authenticity is the path to legacy, and legacy is the music of the extraordinary leader you are meant to be!

Now, the only question left is: Will you choose to say "yes" to being **ALL of YOU** as a leader?

APPENDIX A

LEADERS AND THEIR FAVORITE SONGS

The Extraordinary Book Contributors

Angela Raub	"Fight Song" by Rachel Platten
Amy Balog	"Til Kingdom Come" by Coldplay
Anneka Seely	"California" by Joni Mitchell
Bob Perkins	"Already Gone" by the Eagles
Duane & Kim Cummings	"I Melt with You" by Modern English
Ed Porter	"The Scientist" by Coldplay
James Buckley	"Carry On" by Lost Dog Street Band
John Barrows	"Got to Give It Up" by Marvin Gaye
Katie Rios	"Joyful" by Dante Bowe

Larry Reeves	"Good Day Sunshine" by the Beatles
Laurel Scheaf	"I Left My Heart in San Francisco" by Tony Bennett
Lauren Bailey	"Walking on Sunshine" by Katrina and the Waves
Lori Richardson	"The Climb" by Miley Cyrus
Mark Dougherty	"Blinded by the Light" by Manfred Mann
Meshell Baker	"Lovely Day" by Bill Withers
Michele Kelly	"Cosmic Love" by Florence + the Machine
Rakhi Voria	"Shake It Off" by Taylor Swift
Robert Beattie	"Are You Ready" by AC/DC
Sandra Stosz	"Bohemian Rhapsody" by Queen
Steve Richard	"Question" by the Moody Blues
Tim Rubert	"Tenth Avenue Freeze-Out" by Bruce Springsteen
Tom Dekel	"This Is Why We Fight" by the Decemberists

The Extraordinary Personal Leadership Influencers

Amanda Hammett	"Shake It Off" by Taylor Swift
Amber Villhauer	"Fragments Found" by Fabrizio Paterlini

Anne Sandberg	"Somewhere Over the Rainbow" 1990 rendition by the late Hawaiian singer, Israel Kamakawiwo'ole
Carole Stizza	"I Refuse" by Josh Wilson
Dionne Mischler	"Not Backing Down" by Blanca
Hana Elliot	"Freedom" by Beyoncé
Jeff Plumb	"Simple Man" by Lynyrd Skynyrd
Jennifer Fondervey	"I Want You" by Cheap Trick
Julie Ellis	"Beautiful Day" by U2
Jerry Scher	"You've Got a Friend" by James Taylor
Kris Kelso	"Let It Go" by White Heart
Lauren Allen	"This Is Me" by Keala Settle
Linda White	"We Are Family" by Sister Sledge
Nicole Mahoney	"Jet Airliner" by the Steve Miller Band
Pat O'Donovan	"Different Drum" by the Stone Poneys (featuring Linda Ronstadt)
Phil Blanton	"Best of Me" by Neffex
Rob Bahna	"Badlands" by Bruce Springsteen

| Sharon Preszler | "Waiting on the Weekend" by HARBOUR |
| Tom Schmidt | "Raise a Little Hell" by Trooper |

The Extraordinary Music Contributors & Influencers

Brian Skeel	"A Change of Seasons" by Dream Theater
Cody Carson	"Back Stabbers" by the O'Jays
Maxx Danziger	"Make Your Own Kind of Music" by Cass Elliott

ACKNOWLEDGEMENTS

There are so many people that I am truly honored to have in my life. My husband Mark and our two amazing children, Brad and Becca White. The four people who jumped started this journey: Mark Dougherty, Duane Cummings, Angela Raub, and Amy Balog. All the interview contributors that have brightened my personal and professional life. Lastly, but surely not least, my father, Jud Scheaf, who had the best attitude and perspective on life, and did it all with my extraordinary mother, Virginia Scheaf, and K. Laurel Scheaf, my aunt, who filled in the business piece of my heart when my dad passed away on December 5, 2011.

ABOUT THE AUTHOR

Paula White has an unwavering passion for music and education that she applies to bring new perspectives and open new possibilities for leaders.

A globally recognized sales leader, Paula has leveraged her talents to scale Inside Sales Teams into multi-million standalone sales channels. Paula has also served as a member of the AA-ISP Advisory Board and was previously honored as a Top 25 Most Influential Sales Leader recipient for three consecutive years by AA-ISP.

She has been listed in Ambitions' "Top 100 Coaches to Watch" for two consecutive years in 2017-2018. Currently, Paula is a mentor for #GirlsClub and focuses on fostering the talents of the next generation.

Outside of her work, Paula is an avid concert-goer and has found joy as both a lyricist and a co-producer on six songs. She details the transformative power of this in her book, *Side B*.

Paula's passion for life radiates through all those who work with her. She is a brilliant teacher who draws in the most powerful forces from both halves of the brain and inspires those around her to become truly remarkable in their own ways.